A Mountain Bike Guide to Colorado

≡BICYCLING≡
the Backcountry

William L. Stoehr

Pruett Publishing Co.
Boulder, Colorado

First Edition

2 3 4 5 6 7 8 9

Printed in the United States of America

Book and cover design by Linda Seals

LIBRARY OF CONGRESS CATALOGING-IN-PUBLICATION DATA

Stoehr, William L., 1948-
   Bicycling the backcountry.

   1. Bicycle touring—Colorado—Guide-books.
2. Mountains—Colorado—Recreational use—
Guide-books. 3. Colorado—Description and
travel—1981-   —Guide-books. I. Title.
GV1045.5.C6S76 1987   917.88'0433   87-2363
ISBN 0-87108-725-1 (ppk.)

Contents

To Mary and Greg—
Happy to be here

Holy Mother Earth, the trees and all nature are witness
of your thoughts and deeds.

—A Winnebago Wise Saying

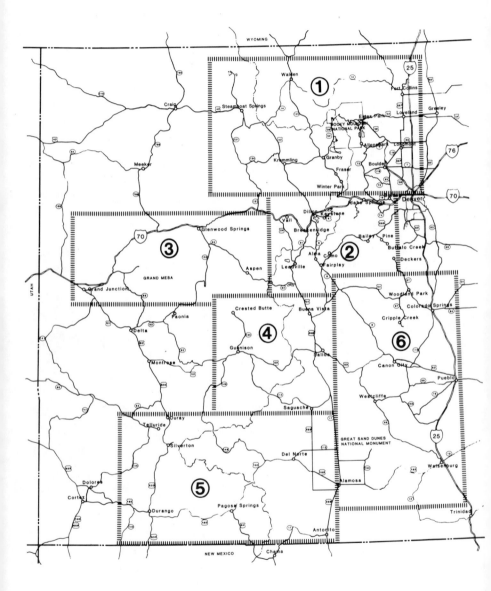

Introduction

Going downhill is the reward for the last two hours of work.
I'm not complaining about the uphill climb; it's just that the
return is special. Your body relaxes, your mind does not. It
seems that increased awareness somehow comes with
increased speed.

The descent from Emerald Lake is typical of what mountain biking can be and is. The years in Colorado still don't
lessen the magic of six feet of snow in July. The wind over the
cold snow and the hot sun react like lead and acid to electrify
your face.

My numb fingers and thumb nudge the right shift lever
through one, two, and three gears as I zoom past Mary and
Greg. I love it. Mountain biking is a lot like cross-country skiing:
the climb, the sweat, the race, the view, the cold, the sun, the
fun.

Mountain biking might be the fastest growing sport in
Colorado. In each of the last four years mountain bike sales
have more than doubled the previous year's sales. In some
areas half of all bikes sold are mountain bikes. The construction
of the bike—the heavy-duty frame, the fat tires, the cantilever
brakes, the additional gears—allows you to go where a ten
speed cannot. The upright riding position is comfortable and
conducive to mountain watching. You might think of a mountain bike as the amalgamation of a lightweight ten-speed racer
and a balloon-tire paperboy bike.

Mountain bikers are to be found on pavement, mining
roads, jeep trails, hiking trails, and dirt. It is their presence on
the last two that is causing dissension. The controversy is over
the use of mountain bikes on public land. Specifically, the key
issues are: the potential for environmental damage, equal access
to recreational areas for mountain bikers, and the aesthetic
impact of mountain bikes on wilderness areas and other trails

where hikers and wildlife are present. With about half of the land in Colorado government owned, and with almost all of the prime recreational land government owned, you can begin to see the problem.

In general, Colorado state, county, and local government roads and trails may be legally used by mountain bikers. The same is true of federally owned land, with the exception of wilderness areas and some National Park trails. In 1964 Congress passed the Wilderness Act, which was intended to preserve certain pristine areas. Section 4(c) of the Wilderness Act prohibits the use of all forms of "mechanical transport" in wilderness areas. The National Forest Service is responsible for the enforcement of the Wilderness Act in twenty-five of Colorado's twenty-eight wilderness areas, and they have interpreted "mechanical transport" to include bicycles. There is also a strong sentiment for further restrictions in areas not covered by the Wilderness Act.

Some people are concerned that mountain bikes will damage our fragile wilderness areas and trails. I suspect that a responsible mountain biker does less damage to a trail than a horse does, yet it can be argued that the issue is one of preventing additional damage of any kind. In other words, if we are to preserve wilderness areas we must minimize our impact on them.

Aesthetic impact is another sticky issue. What this means is that if I am hiking in the woods, I do not want to have you zip by me on a bike. This mechanical intrusion is incongruous with my wilderness experience. For many, preservation of the wilderness experience is the primary reason for the Wilderness Act.

Traditionally the hiker and biker have been of the same ilk. Traditionally both groups have shared a concern for the environment. Traditionally both groups have shared a love for the outdoors. And traditionally both groups have shared an interest in staying in good physical shape. What can be done to resolve this incipient conflict between two such otherwise compatible groups?

One approach is to make mountain bikers aware of the problem, and then provide information regarding attractive alternative mountain bike routes. Hence this book.

Colorado is crisscrossed with a web of backcountry roads, ways, old mining roads, and jeep trails, all available to mountain bikers and leading to some of the most spectacular places on this earth. Many of these places are easily accessed from major population centers. Virtually all of the state's paved, dirt, and two-tread roads are open to mountain bicyclists.

My intent is to outline scenic routes too tough for a ten speed, yet negotiable with a mountain bike. I have attempted to provide a continuum of routes—easy and beginning to strenuous and technically challenging. I have chosen to augment the route descriptions with historical and geological tidbits, plus information regarding trees, flowers, plants, where to fish, and more.

The Basics

How to buy a mountain bike

Not all fat-tire bikes are mountain bikes. A true mountain bike may cost as little as $250 or as much as $3000. Many good mountain bikes fall into the $300 to $600 range. Unless you have a special requirement, or unless you have a burning desire to stimulate the economy, $300 to $600 will get you through most backcountry tours.

The difference between a $300 and a $600 mountain bike may be as tangible as sealed bearings and frame geometry, or as intangible as color and name. But to qualify as a true mountain bike it must have a heavy-duty frame, aluminum wheels, fifteen or more speeds, cantilever or roller cam brakes, and at least 26 X 1.75 fat tires.

Mountain bikes in the $300 to $600 price range typically have a chrome-molybdenum alloy steel frame. This frame is light, yet it has the strength to take the bumps with the flexibility to ease the ride.

Aluminum wheels are lighter than steel, and they provide a better braking surface in wet weather. When it comes to performance, lightweight wheels are more important than a lightweight frame.

Cantilever brakes pull up from both sides of the brake assembly rather than just from the top of the brake. Mechanically speaking, cantilever brakes have a longer lever arm and can apply more force to the pads. Some bikes in the upper end of our price range come with roller cam brakes. Roller cam brakes have a cam plate that pulls up between a set of rollers, forcing the pads against the rim. Here again mechanical advantage is employed to increase braking power. High performance brakes are a safety must if you plan to ride in the hills.

Mountain bikes have a three-gear chainring set versus two for a conventional ten-speed bike. This gives you at least fifteen speeds with some very low gears to get you up steep grades and over rocks. Some come with a six-sprocket rear freewheel cluster for eighteen speeds. Five sprockets give you fifteen speeds. Finally, those fat tires cushion the ride, protect the wheels, and give you increased traction. Fat tire flat tires are rare.

Don't buy the first bike you see. Go for a few rides. Ask if you can at least give the bike a dirt road trial. You are going to spend a lot of money, so be sure to get a bike that fits.

Mountain bike frames are constructed, measured, and sized differently than conventional ten-speed bikes. For starters, you must be able to get both feet flat on the ground without causing yourself permanent physical damage, yet you want to sit and comfortably extend your legs while pedaling. When straddling the mountain bike with both feet flat on the ground, you should have a minimum one-inch clearance over the horizontal bar.

Your handlebars should be level with your seat. In this position you should be able to comfortably reach the handlebars. You will be in a generally upright riding position.

Different bikes have different frame geometry. Frame geometry refers to the relationship of the seat and the front fork to the rest of the frame, the wheelbase length, and the distance between the rear sprocket and the chainring. Geometry affects fit and performance. For most backcountry touring, fit is the most important consideration. Try different frame sizes, adjust the seat and handlebars, and try different makes until you come up with the best combination.

What does more money buy? Sealed bearings for starters. Sealed bearings keep mud, dust, and water out and the grease in. Without sealed bearings you will require additional maintenance. If you plan to ride on dirt roads you may want this feature.

More expensive mountain bikes usually have more expensive brakes, derailleurs, and gears. Depending on your ability, you probably won't be able to tell the difference. If you want your new bike to stay new looking, a chip-resistant chrome finish is a nice touch. If you like the exotic, or if you plan to seriously race, you may want a stiff aluminum or alloy frame. A stiffer frame minimizes frame distortion; it gives you a more efficient but harsher ride.

Get a real mountain bike if you expect to really do mountain biking. Get one that fits if you expect to do it right.

Mountain Biking Precautions and Preparations

I've had a few flat tires on my ten speed; never on my mountain bike. But, I won't let Murphy catch me sans tube and tools. The consequences of a flat are greater in the boonies than on the open road. Make sure you have a spare tube, a pump, and a set of tire irons—those funny little flat bent things.

Mountain bike chain links and derailleurs get bent, and brakes and derailleurs need adjustment at all the wrong times. Minor repairs and adjustments can be made with a few simple tools. I carry various box wrenches, a combination screwdriver, a few allen wrenches, a pair of pliers, a chain link extractor, nuts, bolts, and a few other spare parts. Put together a little tool kit and keep it with your bike. A minor repair can save the day atop Schofield Pass.

Prepare for mountain biking as you would prepare for a hike. Take plenty of water. Your sweat and the dry Colorado air can lead to dehydration. Water can also help you through a mild case of altitude sickness. Many mountain bikes come with braze-ons for a standard pull-top water bottle. Be sure to bring your water and resist the temptation to dip into a cool, clear, natural mountain stream. Streams and lakes may carry the micro-organism Giardia lamblia. Giardiasis can at best give you gas and at worst incapacitate you with diarrhea and severe cramps. Boiling, filtering,or treating the water are the only sure bets.

A first aid kit is a good idea—you are bound to take a spill now and then. Be sure the kit includes a good sunscreen. Don't forget sunglasses, not only at altitude, but anytime it's not dark. Sunglasses make good goggles.

I carry a compass. It's fun to locate landmarks on the map, and it's sometimes critical to figure out where you are. Unmarked roads and confusing intersections are common. If you are unfamiliar with an area, make sure you have a map, preferably a topographic map.

Reflectors are mandatory, and a good bike light is a good idea. I have a generator type light. There are advantages and disadvantages to this style, but I don't want to be caught with dead batteries.

Suit yourself when it comes to kickstands, racks, speedometers, toe clips, quick release hubs, seat locators, and other goodies. You will quickly decide how you want to outfit your bike—just make sure you get stuff that won't rattle off or get knocked off. I'm risking it with my generator light.

Think about what you wear. I like to ride in shorts six months out of the year. I have also been caught in shorts on Boreas when it was snowing. Plan for Colorado mountain weather and elevation changes. Don't forget how hot you can get pedaling up and how cold you can get cruising down. Layer your clothes.

Wear a helmet. It's mandatory for sanctioned events for a good reason. Padded gloves cushion shock, and padded pants reduce chafing. There is a good chance that you will be walking some of the time; wear shoes that you can hike in.

With Rocky Mountain summers come Rocky Mountain afternoon thunderstorms—hail, lightning, and driving rain. Start early and pack a poncho.

Be prepared for the worst in weather or whatever. Be prepared to spend the night. On a long ride into the back-country make sure you have a way to stay warm, a way to fix your bike, and a way to treat minor injuries.

This is not necessarily scientific, but many experienced riders will tell you that 25 miles on a dirt road is as hard as 50 on pavement. Remember this when planning a tour.

Always be sure you know what the trail conditions are before you ride. Snow, mud, or rock slides occasionally block high mountain trails. When in doubt, call the local Forest Service district office.

Skills and Thrills

Let's assume that you know how to mount and pedal a bike. If you're just going to ride around town you can stop here. If not, read on.

The best way to learn to ride a mountain bike is to ride a mountain bike. Learning to control a skid or to anticipate a hazard comes with experience—but there are some things I can tell you.

Keep your weight forward on inclines. Tipping over backwards will be an object lesson in the importance of weight distribution. Lean forward and hunch down over your handlebars when going up. There is a fine line between keeping your front wheel on the ground and still maintaining traction with the rear. If you need to stand up to pedal, then shift up to a higher gear so that you have some crank resistance. This will help you keep your balance. The problem with standing is that you are more apt to spin your rear wheel. The advantage is that you can generate more climbing power. When standing, crouch forward to keep your front wheel down, and stick your butt out over the bike seat to keep weight on your rear wheel for increased traction.

When approaching a hill, don't shift down too soon. Give yourself a running start and then drop down to a lower gear, but shift to a lower gear while you still have momentum. Shifting while straining to go uphill doesn't work. Your derailleur will only shift gears when it is lightly loaded. If you are climbing and you need to shift to a lower gear, unload your derailleur by pedaling faster for a few seconds to gain a bit of momentum, ease up, and then shift.

Cross-gear shifts frequently won't work, and they are hard on your gears and chain. A cross-gear shift refers to an attempt to run the chain between your small front chain ring and one of your smaller rear freewheel sprockets, or vice-versa. Sometimes this cannot be avoided, but when you find that your chain just won't climb over a gear, reduce the tension on it by moving the other end to a middle gear.

Lower your bike seat when making steep descents. This

lowers your center of gravity and eliminates that falling-over-forward feeling. It also puts you in a better position to pick your way through rough terrain—as long as you do not have to do much pedaling. A real mountain bike comes with a quick-release seatpost lock; no need for a wrench.

When you ride rough stuff, time your pedal rotations to clear rocks and other obstacles. When going downhill, avoid hitting smaller obstructions by cruising with the pedal cranks parallel to the ground. Catching a pedal hurts.

Watch for loose gravel. On back roads loose gravel is frequently deep gravel. You don't need to avoid it—just be careful in it. Deep loose gravel can throw you off balance.

As you do when skiing moguls, learn to choose a line. Look ahead and pick your way through the obstacles. As you get better and braver you'll want to bounce off a few, but for now take it easy and learn to control your bike.

Be careful with your front brakes. A quick way to go head over handlebars is to lock your front wheel when going fast or down a grade. Forward weight transfer occurs during braking. When your weight moves over your front wheel, your front brakes become more effective. Be safe; use both brakes when you can.

Get in the habit of keeping at least your thumb and forefinger wrapped around the handlebar grip when riding in rubble. You can still brake with your remaining fingers. But hitting a rock or rut can jerk the handlebars out of your hands if you don't have a good grip.

Get up off your seat and push off on the pedals when going over bumps. Let your legs absorb the shock. When you can't avoid a rock or a log, or when you don't want to avoid it, learn to tranfer your weight to the rear tire, push hard on your pedals, and lift your front wheel up over the obstacle. Then transfer your weight forward and unweight the rear wheel as you complete your hop. Keep your weight off the wheel that is making contact with an obstacle,

It's fun to bounce down a four-wheel-drive trail at twenty miles per hour, but you better know what you are doing. Be alert. Keep a safe distance between riders. Ride under control.

Very Simple Maintenance and Care

I like to do minor adjustments, replace brake pads, and fix bent things. I leave the tough stuff to a bicycle mechanic. Suit yourself and your pocketbook in this regard.

Something we can all do is to wash our bikes after a muddy ride. Dirt, mud, and dust cause unnecessary drive train wear, encourage squeaks, and contribute to sluggish gear changes. Be careful in the car wash. High-pressure sprays can drive water into your bearings, doing more harm than good. After a wash, spray your chain, gears, and derailleurs with bike lube or silicon.

Bouncing off rocks loosens things. It seems that mountain bike bolts and nuts require constant attention. Be sure to check your headset, brakes, shifters, and spokes before you take a major ride.

Using the Route Descriptions

You can select your route by consulting the state route location map, or you can pick it from one of the appendicies. Appendix 1 is a tabulation of the rides by ride rating: easy, moderate, and strenuous. Appendix 2 is a tabulation of eighty "other" routes, recommended but not described in this book.

Each of the route descriptions has two ratings. The RIDE RATING is a composite rating that takes into account the physical strength and endurance required. It also indirectly takes into account the level of skill needed. The ratings are based on normal route conditions—snow, mud, or water could dramatically change a route.

A more technical ride will generally require more strength and endurance. A beginning or intermediate ride can also be strenuous if there is a long climb.

You can make an easy ride strenuous if you really push it. A strenuous ride can be moderate if you walk the hard parts. Whether you are a beginner or an old pro, don't be afraid of any of the routes—just be aware of what you are getting into and plan accordingly.

Each ride also has a SKILL LEVEL RATING: beginning, intermediate, or advanced. I would rate an all-weather gravel road with some ruts and moderate inclines as a beginning tour; no particular mountain biking skills are required. A four-wheel-drive trail with rocks, obstructions, and 40 percent grades would merit an advanced rating. Intermediate is somewhere in between. You'll soon get the hang of it.

Frequently a route will start out easy and beginning only to end up strenuous and advanced. I will point this out so you can decide if you only want to do part of a route. If a large part of the ride is advanced, I will rate it advanced. But if a beginning route has a short advanced section, I may still call the route easy and assume you can walk the hard part.

The ride and skill ratings are quite subjective, and probably tainted by the weather and the amount of sleep I got the night before. I have tried to make adjustments. Beginners can be assured that an easy/beginning ride is about as easy as you can get.

TRIP MILEAGE is approximate. I used a bicycle speedometer/odometer, rounded off the tenths, and attempted to account for a few route diversions. Ride time is just as approximate. Remember, stronger, more skillful bikers will go faster. RIDE TIME means time in the saddle. On a one-way ride, ride time is the time it takes to ride on your bike from point A to point B. Lunch, fishing, and wildflower identification time is not included. After a few rides you will be better able to estimate your own time.

Because you will generally be biking on a road, you can change the trip mileage by parking and starting in a different place. But if a route is on a four-wheel-drive road, don't try it in your VW.

I have indicated the STARTING ELEVATION and the HIGHEST POINT on each route. The elevation changes are shown on the elevation/distance graph. This graph approximates a cross section of the terrain for a given route. Elevations are taken from altimeter readings and topographic maps. Unless I was able to pinpoint an exact elevation location, I rounded elevations off.

You should be able to get to a route with the Colorado area map, and you should be able to pedal the route with the topographical MAP and description provided in this book.

However, you may decide to explore an alternative route, and maps are fun, so you may want to take one or more along. I like the Trails Illustrated series of topo maps; they cover more area than a USGS quad, they are waterproof, tearproof, and they pack well. I like them so much, in fact, that my wife and I bought the company. They can be cross-referenced with the USGS maps and picked up at your favorite sports equipment store.

A topo map describes terrain in intervals as shown by contour lines. Each line represents a given altitude. The darker index lines are marked with the altitude. The lighter intermediate lines represent in-between altitude gradations. A typical USGS 7.5-minute topographic map has forty-foot contour intervals. At a glance, close index lines mean steep grades.

In the text, I describe inclines in terms of percent grade rather than in degrees. Percent grade is the method of expressing vertical drop that you usually see on ski slopes and highways. Moguls typically start to form on a 40 percent slope; I think you get the idea.

I have described these routes as they where in 1986. Some things may have changed. It is your responsibility to be aware of change, and it is your responsibility to be prepared for a given mountain bike ride.

Rides in Zone 1

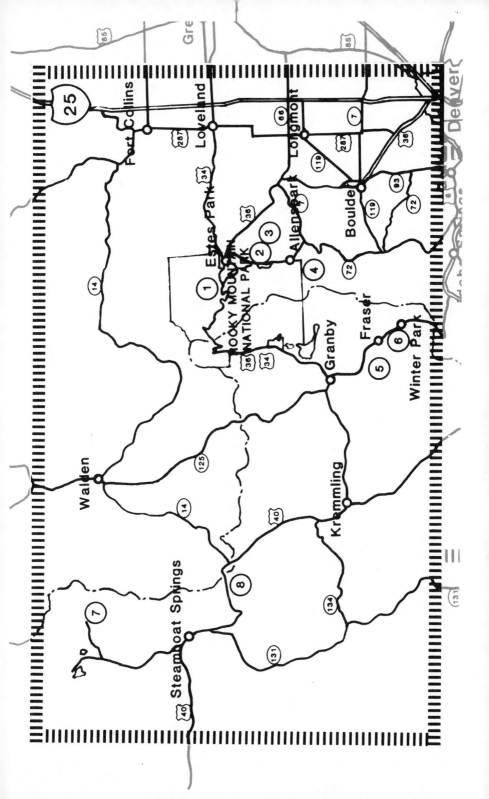

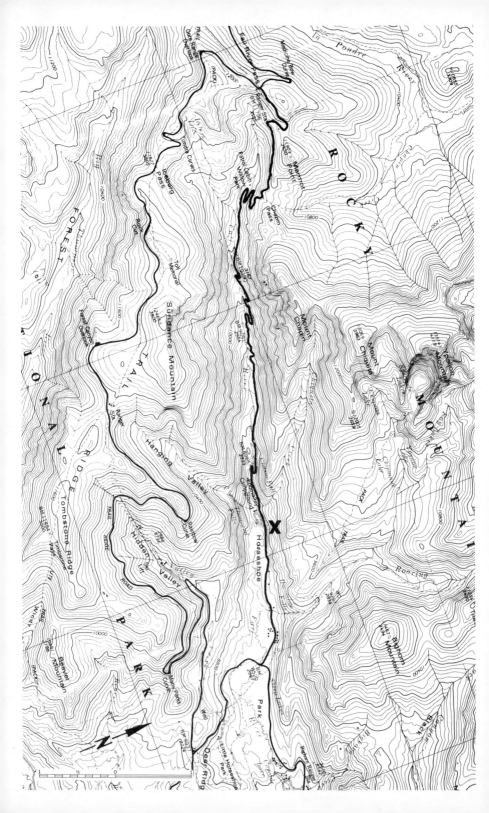

Old Fall River Road Loop **1**

RIDE RATING: Moderate/Strenuous
SKILL LEVEL: Beginning
ROUND TRIP: 32 miles
APPROXIMATE RIDE TIME: 4 hours
STARTING ELEVATION: 8590 feet
HIGHEST POINT: 12,180 feet
MAPS: Roosevelt National Forest
      USGS 7.5 Minute Estes Park, Trail Ridge, Fall River Pass
      USGS Rocky Mountain National Park

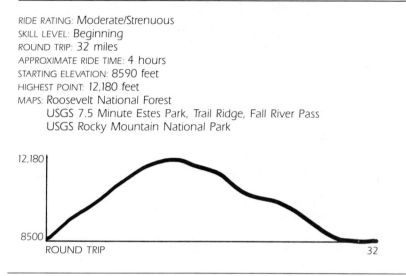

12,180

8500

ROUND TRIP   32

Before there was Trail Ridge Road, there was Fall River Road. Conceived in 1912, completed in 1920, constructed by convicts, Fall River Road is the original transmountain highway through Rocky Mountain National Park. It is the only unpaved mountain bike route in the national park. You can ride on the other roads, it's just that this one is gravel. Your return is on Trail Ridge Road. Trail Ridge is paved, almost all downhill, and scenic. This route return is worth a ride rather than a shuttle.

Fall River Road is a 9.5-mile one-way uphill climb. It is open to mountain bikes and motorized vehicles, starting the fourth of July. Start early to avoid traffic. If you slept in, go anyway—it's great. The cars will be going slowly, and in the same direction you are. The Moderate/Strenuous ride rating is only because of the constant 10-20 percent grade. You will be stopping frequently for the view, so there will be plenty of time to rest. It will be hard to get lost on this ride. Don't worry about a detailed map—the standard park issue will be just fine.

Enter Rocky Mountain National Park at the Fall River Entrance Station. After about 2 miles, turn right at Sheep Lake and head for the Endovalley picnic area. You can park at the picnic area or at the Fall River Road parking area. There are markers along the road that identify points of interest. Spring for the two bits and get one of the trail guides from the vending machine at the start.

The road rises out of Horseshoe Park Meadow, a glacier-formed valley. The views are spectacular. There is so much evidence of change that you can somehow feel it happening.

A Fall River Road ride is a lesson in geography as you pass through three life zones. As you start out in the montane zone you will see a mixture of lodgepole pine, Douglas fir, Engelmann spruce, aspen, subalpine fir, and a tree you don't see that often, limber pine. There is thimbleberry all along the road.

You are likely to see many wildflowers. One of my favorites, the shooting star, likes this place. After a mile, look to your left at the north face of the ridge and you can see the damage to the trees caused by insects.

Be alert for animals. As we gained elevation, we saw many Clark's nutcrackers, a couple of marmots, heard our share of pikas, and even saw a bobcat.

In the beginning, the marbled mountain in front of you is Mount Chapin. Mount Chapin is in the Mummy Range section of the northern Front Range.

The climate subtly changes from montane to subalpine at around 2 miles, and the Engelmann spruce becomes the predominant tree. The road does not change. It is still, and will continue to be, a good road. The views are great the entire route.

At about 7 miles the trees start to thin out as you approach the timberline and the alpine zone. High wind, low temperature, heavy snow, and inconsistent moisture combine to discourage the trees. If you are not from Colorado you will probably want to stop and have someone take a picture of you in the snow.

Fall River Pass (11,796 feet) and the Alpine Visitor Center are at just over 9 miles. Remember, Fall River Road is one-way. Make a left onto paved Trail Ridge Road, pedal 1.5 miles up to the Gore Range Overlook (12,183 feet), and then revel in the 18-mile descent to Sheep Lake. Turn left at Sheep Lake and head back to where you parked.

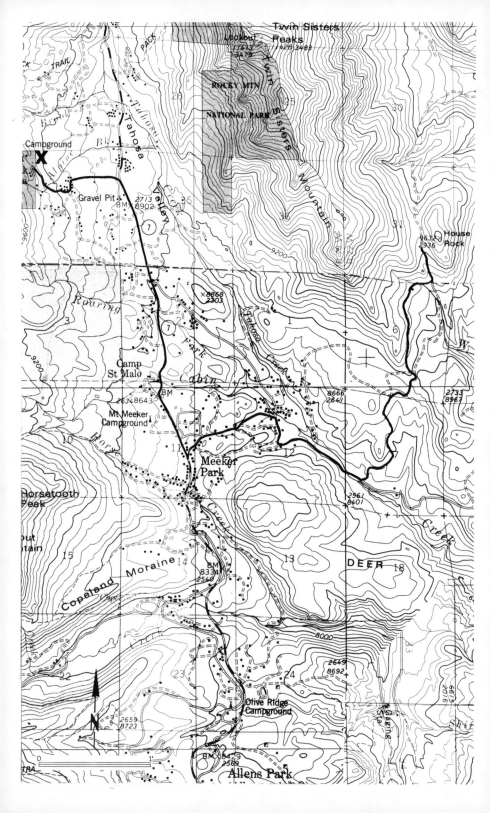

RIDE RATING: Strenuous
SKILL LEVEL: Intermediate
ROUND TRIP: 22 miles
APPROXIMATE RIDE TIME: 4 hours
STARTING ELEVATION: 9300 feet
HIGHEST POINT: 9300 feet
MAPS: Roosevelt National Forest
USGS 7.5 Minute Longs Peak, Allens Park, Raymond,
Panorama Peak

9300
8400
ROUND TRIP   22

Don't misinterpret the route summary; this one is neither flat
nor all downhill. It goes down and up and down and up. The
first 7 miles are relatively easy, so you may wish to simply do
the first part.

With good camping so close, think about staying in Rocky
Mountain National Park, or in the Roosevelt National Forest,
and knocking off a few of the routes around Estes Park. If you
unpacked your gear at the Longs Peak campground, go south
less than 4 miles toward Meeker Park on Colorado Hwy. 7, past
the Roosevelt National Forest picnic grounds, and left on Cabin
Creek Road, Boulder County Hwy. 82.

You will ride through a private residential area, and then at
about 5.5 miles you'll come up to an unmarked intersection
where you turn right and continue east on Boulder County
Hwy. 82. The road follows Cabin Creek, where the elevation
drops under 8000 feet. This is a wetland area, a red-winged
blackbird bivouac. Dive-bombing raids aside, I love red-wings;
they somehow take me back to another time.

After less than 7 miles there is a sign for House Rock, Estes
Park, and Pierson Park. Follow the arrows left and head up and
north. You will quickly enter the Roosevelt National Forest.
From this point the route get tougher, starting with a 30

percent grade as you turn up the road. It's pretty much a continuous climb from here. You will pick up 1300 feet over the next 3 miles.

The road is a four-wheel-drive road with ruts, rocks, and loose stones. The higher you go the worse it gets. There are some good camping spots along the road, and to the west, a view of Longs Peak that will knock your socks off.

After 8 miles you are up around 9000 feet and still climbing. To the south is a view of Longs Peak (14,256 feet) and Mt. Meeker (13,911 feet). These two mountains were once known as The Two Ears by the French, and as The Two Guides by the Arapaho. Major Stephen D. Long led an expedition into Colorado in 1819. When he had this mountain named after him, the U.S. Board of Geographic Names decided to drop the apostrophe in Long's. Nathan C. Meeker was one of the founders of Greeley. Later he was an agent at the White River Ute Indian Agency, and in 1879 Meeker and the other agency employees were massacred by Indians. Now we have Mt. Meeker, Meeker Park, Meeker Ridge, and the town of Meeker.

Back on the road again, at 8.5 miles there is a Pierson Park sign. Make a left and go north on Pierson Park Road. In about a mile you will come to a gate straight ahead and House Rock to the right. This is the turnaround point for this tour. If you are still game, open the gate and continue to Pierson Park. Please close the gate after you go through. The road gets quite bad and the descent is quite steep. From this point it is 3 miles to Pierson Park, and 7 to Estes Park.

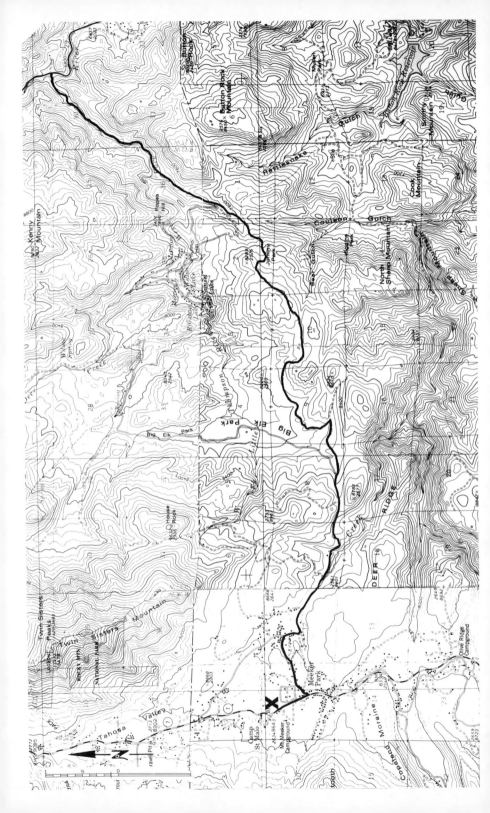

Johnny Park 3

RIDE RATING: Moderate/Strenuous
SKILL LEVEL: Advanced
ONE WAY: 12 miles
APPROXIMATE ONE-WAY RIDE TIME: 3 hours
STARTING ELEVATION: 8600 feet
HIGHEST POINT: 8600 feet
MAPS: Roosevelt National Forest
    USGS 7.5 Minute Allens Park, Raymond, Panorama Peak,
    Pinewood Lake

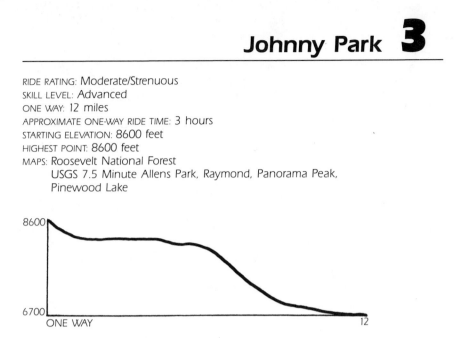

You can walk the hard parts; but then you better add an hour or so to the ride time. This is a challenging mountain bike route for the advanced rider, yet makable by an intermediate. This description covers a one-way ride from Meeker Park through Johnny Park to U.S. Hwy. 36. There are a few alternative ways to approach this tour. You can shuttle a car. You can do a grand loop through Estes Park. Or you can go over and back. In each case you can follow this narrative.

Park and unload in the Meeker Park National Forest picnic ground 8 miles south of Estes Park on Colorado Hwy. 7. Pedal less than a mile south on 7 to Cabin Creek Road, Boulder County Hwy. 82, and head east, left, on an all-weather gravel road. You will ride through a private residential area and then up to an unmarked intersection where you turn right and continue east on 82 along Cabin Creek.

After less than 3 miles you will see a sign for Estes Park, House Rock, and Pierson Park; don't turn, forge ahead and enter the Roosevelt National Forest. Soon you will see the sign for Johnny Park Road; turn right and prepare to open your first

25

gate. Don't worry; you're not trespassing. Forest Service roads frequently cross private land. Private landowners may have cattle that they would prefer not get out—please shut the gate behind you. The road is a rutted dirt road and relatively easy to ride. Between 4 and 5 miles there is a nice meadow. I saw lots of elk sign in this area, plus columbines as thick as I have ever seen them.

This may come as a shock, but you can't always rely on maps. The national forest map does not show a continuous road to Johnny Park. Trust me, it does go through.

Up to this point the route has been relatively easy; moderate grades, and a rutted road at worst. Now you will encounter rocks and washed-out areas that will challenge your riding ability.

There is a good Rocky Mountain National Park view at 5 to 6 miles followed by a short 35-40 percent incline. After 6 miles there is another gate, and beyond it is 100 yards of very rough, slick, and steep (30 percent) terrain. If you walk

anywhere it will probably be here. It does gets relatively better, but not much. In another 1 mile there is a great view. To the east you can probably see Kansas, and to the southwest snowcapped peaks. Soon you'll be heading down. It's still rough, but it's 1 mile or so downhill into Johnny Park. You can camp in Johnny Park.

At 9 miles there is an intersection of three roads and a sign that tells you where you have been. Turn left to a civilized gravel road. Follow this road and the cottonwood-lined Little Thompson River for an uneventful 4 miles to U.S. Hwy. 36.

As discussed above, you can turn left and take Hwy. 36 into Estes Park, you can go back the way you came, or if you shuttled a car you can rest.

Here's a bit of trivia for you if you are heading to Estes Park. You probably know that Estes Park is the primary east entrance to Rocky Mountain National Park. Not long after Joel Estes settled in this valley, Estes Park became a tourist town and in the 1870s home to Colorado's first dude ranch. In 1910 the Stanley Hotel opened, and in 1915 Congress "created" Rocky Mountain National Park.

Just before you reach town you pass Lake Estes, a man-made lake resulting from a U.S. Deptartment of the Interior-Bureau of Reclamation hydo-generation project. This facility generates electricity and sends it to another government agency for distribution to electric utilities.

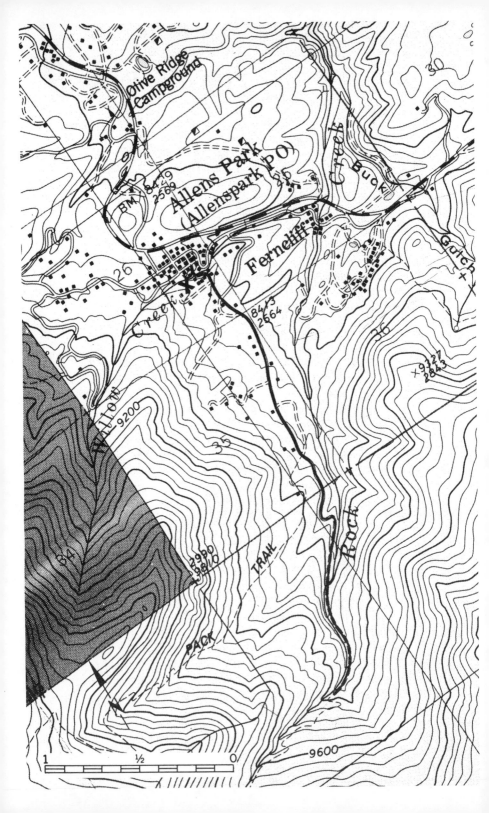

Rock Creek Ski Road **4**

RIDE RATING: Moderate
SKILL LEVEL: Intermediate
ROUND TRIP: 6 miles
APPROXIMATE RIDE TIME: 1 hour
STARTING ELEVATION: 8350 feet
HIGHEST POINT: 9100 feet
MAPS: Roosevelt National Forest
     USGS 7.5 Minute Allens Park
     USGS Rocky Mountain National Park

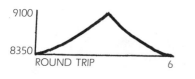

9100

8350

ROUND TRIP   6

Rock Creek Ski Road is near the southeast corner of Rocky Mountain National Park. If you are coming back from a ride in the Estes Park area craving just 6 more miles, try this one. To get there from Estes Park, take Colorado Hwy. 7 south to Allenspark, a quaint little town away from the miniature golf courses. In 1864 the prospector Alonzo Allen built a cabin some 2 miles from this namesake of his.

Park in Allenspark and pedal over to Boulder County 107, located about midway through town. If you are coming from the north it's on the right side of the road. Boulder County 107 starts out as an all-weather gravel road with moderate rolling grades. In less than .5 miles bear left, keep pedaling, and enter the Roosevelt National Forest at 1.2 miles. At about 1.5 miles go left on Rock Creek Ski Road, Forest Route 116. From here the road becomes a relatively rocky four-wheel-drive route.

At this elevation the trees are predominantly Engelmann spruce and subalpine fir. These two trees form the climax forest of the upper montane life zone. They extend from the montane, through the subalpine, and into the alpine zones. St. Louis physician and botanist, Dr. George Engelmann, first came to Colorado in 1874. Engelmann and his associates named many Colorado plants and land forms; today we have

Engelmann canyon, peak, rose, daisy, aster, and of course spruce.

There is a campsite along Rock Creek at 2 miles, and they tell me that there are trout in Rock Creek. This road is the access to what was to be the Rock Creek Ski Area. The Forest Service once studied the area for ski hill potential. Apparently someone was counting chickens when they named the road. Anyhow, continue up a moderate incline until you reach the end of the main road at 3 miles. Turn around and go back the way you came.

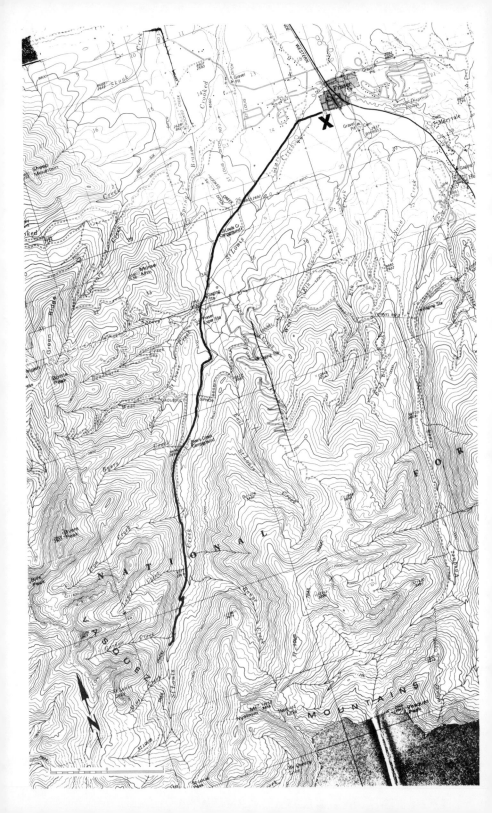

St. Louis Creek/Fraser Experimental Forest **5**

RIDE RATING: Easy/Moderate
SKILL LEVEL: Beginning
ROUND TRIP: 25 miles
APPROXIMATE RIDE TIME: 3 hours
STARTING ELEVATION: 8550 feet
HIGHEST POINT: 10,300 feet
MAPS: Arapaho National Forest
      USGS 7.5 Minute Fraser, Bottle Pass, Byers Peak

The last time you were in the Fraser Experimental Forest you were probably putting wax on those skinny boards of yours. Not only is this a good place to cross-country ski, it is also a good beginning mountain bike route.

Take U.S. 40 to the center of downtown Fraser. There is a sign on the west side of U.S. 40 at Eisenhaur Drive proclaiming that Fraser is the icebox of the nation. Turn west onto Eisenhaur Drive, continue to the end of Eisenhaur, then turn left onto Carriage Road. Carriage Road ends at County Road 73, the Fraser Experimental Forest Road. Turn right onto 73, park along the road, and start pedaling toward the Fraser Experimental Forest.

The road is a good, rolling, all-weather gravel road. There is some traffic on this road; most of it is on the first part of the ride.

As you start out, you are in an open area with great views in all directions. In the summer you can expect to see lupine, scarlet gilia, elephanthead, yellow paintbrush, stonecrop, columbine, and more.

About 2 miles from Fraser you'll enter the Fraser Experimental Forest. This forest is part of the Arapaho National

Forest, and it is a proving ground for silvaculture techniques such as tree thinning. Camping is restricted to designated areas.

The road gently climbs south along St. Louis Creek, which contains rainbow, brook, and cutthroat trout. It is stocked.

As you approach 7 miles there is a side road and a sign for the Byers Creek Campground. This may be a little confusing; keep to the right. After this point the road becomes rougher and steeper with a short 10 percent climb followed by a more moderate incline for most of the way.

Above 9000 feet, watch the area change into a predominantly Engelmann spruce and subalpine fir forest. Heartleaf arnica and Parry primrose start to show up at this altitude.

At about 12 miles you cross Mine Creek. From here the road again gets rockier and steeper. The ride is getting more difficult, but it is still very makable for a beginner.

The road ends at 12.5 miles. You may wish to park your bike under a tree, grab your lunch, and hike up one of the trails that starts at the end of the road. You can reach St. Louis Peak, Lake, and Pass from this point. It's a 3-mile hike to St. Louis Lake, a four-acre lake at 11,400 feet with a few cutthroats.

The easy descent back to Fraser is fun. The view to Devils Thumb and the great divide is great.

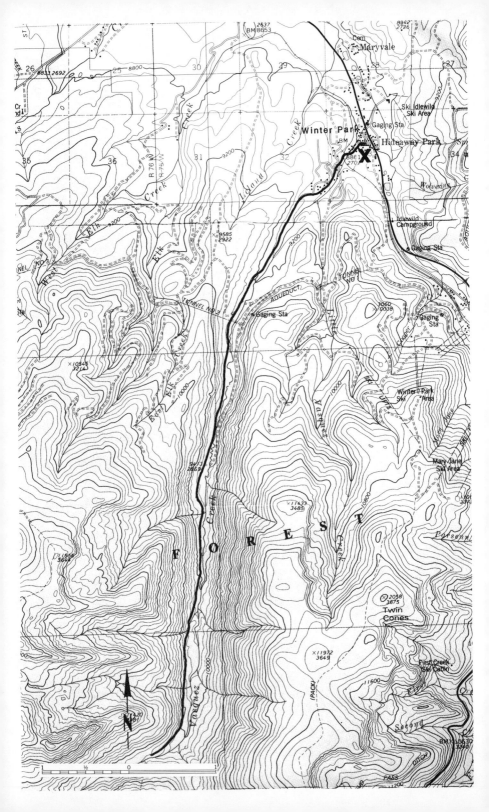

Vasquez Creek 6

RIDE RATING: Easy/Moderate
SKILL LEVEL: Intermediate
ROUND TRIP: 17 miles
APPROXIMATE RIDE TIME: 3 hours
STARTING ELEVATION: 8750 feet
HIGHEST POINT: 10,000 feet
MAPS: Arapaho National Forest
    USGS 7.5 Minute Fraser, Berthoud Pass

Starting in Winter Park, this route takes you up and down Vasquez Creek. The first 5 miles of this route are relatively easy.

Take U.S. Hwy. 40 to Winter Park. From the southern side of the main downtown area, go west on Vasquez Road and park in the Winter Park municipal parking garage/lot.

Pedal west on paved Vasquez Road past condos, inns, and private residences. At about 1 mile the main paved road turns right. Don't go right; go straight, climb a 10 percent hill, and ride into the Arapaho National Forest. You will find some good camping along the creek. There are a few side roads along the way. Don't be afraid to explore; it's hard to get lost in this valley.

The road is rocky enough to keep your attention, yet easy enough for a beginner. The elevation gain is very moderate all along the first part of the route. Willow-lined Vasquez Creek will be to your left the entire trip up the valley. Unless it has been recently stocked, or unless you want to practice keeping a hares ear out of your hair, forget about fishing; it's not a hot spot. Elephanthead likes cold mountain streams; watch for this nifty wildflower.

At 2.5 miles you are still climbing, but you can probably keep pedaling 8 miles per hour all day. There are many shallow depressions in the road, and they quickly turn into lakes after a rain. If it has rained in the last day, plan on getting wet. Puddles are a blast to tear through. There's nothing like fat tires and a puddle to take you back a few years.

There is a sign at 2.8 miles warning you of a narrow road and blind curves; you are headed the right way. There is some traffic on this road. Be alert.

There is a dam at 4.5 miles and a road over a bridge that will take you back down the other side of the Vasquez. Unless you want to head back, go straight and on to what becomes a four-wheel-drive road.

If you have not already noticed, the forest is now populated with spruce, lodgepole pine, and fir. You are up around 9500 feet and getting into the subalpine climate zone.

Around 6 miles the road gets rougher and steeper. There is a steady 20 percent grade followed by a short very steep climb. You beginners will probably walk this one. The challenge of a steep hill is to combine strength and endurance with skill. Distribute your weight to keep your front wheel on the ground and your rear wheel biting into the gravel.

Twenty-percent climbs and a rocky road are the norm for the next couple of miles. There is a narrow log bridge over the creek at 6.8 miles. Consider walking your bike over it.

At 7.5 miles, in the summer of 1986, the road was washed out. I carried my bike over the rushing water and then watched a four-wheel-drive vehicle fail to make it over. His problem was the steep bank on the other side; no problem on foot. In the future expect a repaired road and culvert.

The road is narrow and overgrown until you ride into a large open area at 8.5 miles. This is the end. There is a continental divide view. To the south is Vasquez Pass and Stanley Mountain. West of the pass is Vasquez Peak. There is a hiking trail to the left that goes up to Vasquez Pass. A four-wheel-drive road continues for a half mile or so to the right.

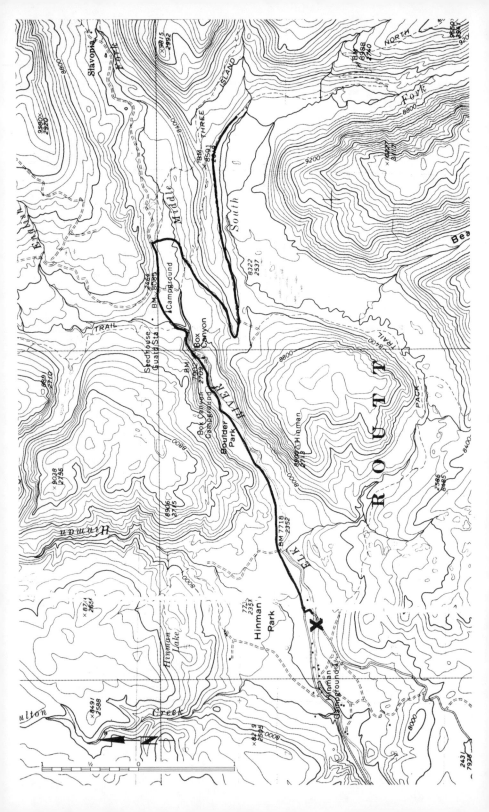

Seedhouse Road 7

RIDE RATING: Easy
SKILL LEVEL: Beginning
ROUND TRIP: 16 miles
APPROXIMATE RIDE TIME: 2 hours
STARTING ELEVATION: 7680 feet
HIGHEST POINT: 8450
MAPS: Routt National Forest
     USGS 7.5 Minute Farwell Mountain, Mount Zirkel

This is one of many easy mountain bike routes north of Steamboat Springs. To get there take U.S. Hwy. 40 west for about 2 miles out of Steamboat Springs to the Elk River Road turnoff, which is also Routt County 129. Make a right turn and head north on 129, proceed past the airport, and continue for about 25 miles to Forest Route 400, Seedhouse Road. Seedhouse Road is just on the north side of Glen Eden. Turn right onto Seedhouse Road and continue for about 6 more miles through Hinman Park and to the Hinman Campground turnoff at Forest Route 440, Reed Creek Road. Park in the open area along the road, unload your bike, get back out on Seedhouse Road and continue up the road toward Slavonia. As you pedal up the road you will see several campsites.

In the winter this is a good place to cross-country ski. The county plows Seedhouse Road up to the Hinman Campground turnoff. Don't bring your light carbons; there are no set trails. Seedhouse Road runs along the Elk River, which is fast moving and turbulent. It produces rainbow, brook, cutthroat, and brown trout. It is also occasionally stocked. The Elk River watershed is a high-production area; it produces enough water to meet the annual needs of a half million people.

The road is all-weather gravel. Begin pedaling up a gentle incline through Boulder Park at 1.7 miles and into the Box Canyon area around 2.5 miles. Note the subtle change in the trees as aspen and lodgepole pine start to dominate the forest. On a summer ride you can expect to see a good variety of wildflowers. At 3.5 miles cross the bridge over the north fork of the Elk River and continue past the Seedhouse Campground. The Seedhouse guard station is to your left. This was once a Forest Service cone collection station where seeds for tree propagation were accumulated, sorted, and saved.

At 4 miles the ride is still gentle as you pass Lost Dog Road on your left and begin a moderate descent. At 4.3 miles turn right onto Forest Route 443 and cross over the middle fork of the Elk River. Seedhouse Road continues another couple of miles to Slavonia. Slavonia, an old mining community, served the Slavonia Mine; you way wish to add mileage to this ride and check it out.

Keep climbing 443. At 5.8 miles there is a side road to the right (don't take it) and a good view of the Sawtooth Range. Forest Route 1100 is on the right at 6.1 miles; it leads to the Mount Zirkel Wilderness. Stay on 443 and continue along the south fork of the Elk River.

At around 7.5 miles the gravel road turns to a dirt road, and at 8 miles it ends in a turnaround. Turn around and head back.

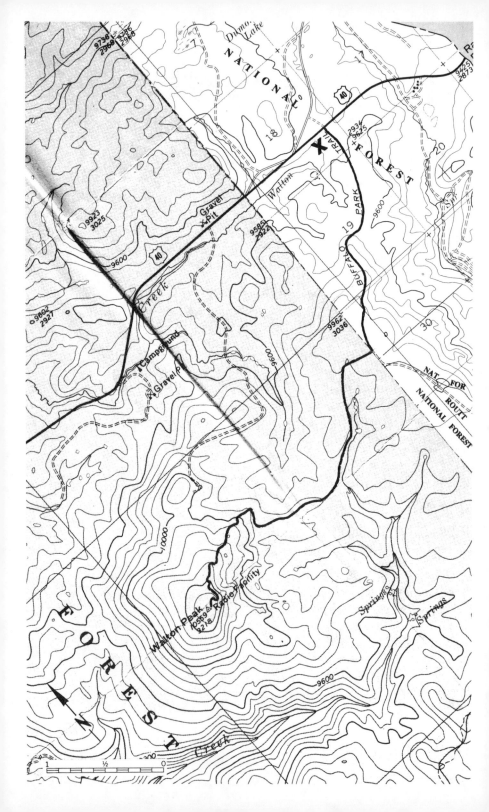

RIDE RATING: Moderate/Strenuous
SKILL LEVEL: Intermediate
ROUND TRIP: 12.5 miles
APPROXIMATE RIDE TIME: 2.5 hours
STARTING ELEVATION: 9559 feet
HIGHEST POINT: 10,559 feet
MAPS: Routt National Forest
    USGS 7.5 Minute Mount Werner, Walton Peak

This route takes you to the radio relay station at the top of Walton Peak. Walton Peak is in the Park Range and south of Rabbit Ears Pass. The road to the top is an adequate primitive road. This means that it is not something you would want to take the new family sedan on, but a jeep would do just fine.

This entire Rabbit Ears Pass area is a great place to cross-country ski. I have skied this particular section, and I remember it as both sunny and hot, and windy and cold—typical Colorado touring.

From Steamboat Springs, take U.S. Hwy. 40 toward Rabbit Ears Pass. Drive past the Walton Creek Campground and continue for a mile or so to Forest Route 251. The sign says Dumont Lake and Harrison Creek. Make a right turn onto 251, park along the road, hop on your bike, and follow the sign toward Harrison Creek.

Starting out on a very rutted dirt road, head south and up a mild incline. This area has a very open feeling to it. There is a mixture of lodgepole pine, subalpine fir, and Engelmann spruce as you move through this ecosystem transitional area. In summer you will see lupine, Indian paintbrush, cow parsnip, and gilia.

To the rear you can see the Rabbit Ears Range along with Rabbit Ears Peak. The distinctive earred summit of Rabbit Ears Peak is the top of a volcanic plug, a lava-filled feeder pipe of an old volcano. Volcanic mountains are not as common in Colorado as are faulted anticlines like the Front and Park ranges.

At less than a mile there is a brief 20 percent incline. There is also a road to the left; don't take it—continue straight. There is a campsite loop with a grand view at 1.5 miles. Continue to pedal up the mild incline until you reach the turn for Walton Peak at 2.2 miles. The sign says Buffalo Park straight ahead and Walton Peak to the right. Turn right on Forest Route 251. Descend into an open meadow and proceed toward Walton Peak. The road gets progressively worse. Be alert.

At 3.75 miles climb a 20-25 percent hill. At 4.5 miles the climb is easier, but that doesn't last long as you run up against a 40 percent section. The road goes from dirt to rock at 4.75 miles, while you continue to climb.

There is a little loop in the road just before a great lookout at 6 miles. From the lookout you can see 180 degrees east to

west, with views of the snowcapped mountains of the Gore Range to the southeast. This is the place to eat your lunch. Spruce and fir are the dominant tree species at this elevation.

The end of the road is at 6.25 miles. At the top there is a large radio relay station used by the state highway people.

Return the same way you came. Be careful as you head back down the mountain. It's easy to let your mind wander. It's easy to build up speed real fast. It's easy to hit a rock or a rut and lose control. But it sure is fun.

Rides in Zone 2

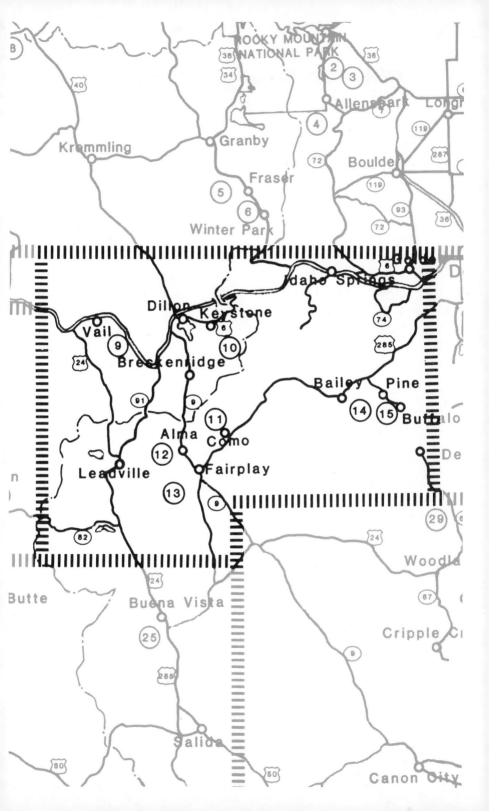

Vail Pass to Redcliff 9

RIDE RATING: Strenuous
SKILL LEVEL: Intermediate
ROUND TRIP: 23.5 miles
APPROXIMATE RIDE TIME: 4 hours
STARTING ELEVATION: 10,600 feet
HIGHEST POINT: 11,156 feet
MAPS: Arapaho National Forest, White River National Forest
   USGS 7.5 Minute Vail Pass, Red Cliff

11,156

8800

ROUND TRIP   23.5

This one takes you from Vail Pass over Shrine Pass to Redcliff.
This is a good mountain bike ride. This is also a popular
weekend car ride, so watch for traffic. In the winter this is a
prime ski tour route.

Most of the ride to Redcliff is downhill. If you are not up
for the strenuous return trip you may want to shuttle a car. The
above route summary covers a round trip.

The Mount of the Holy Cross dominates the view for part
of the route. I don't know what it is about this mountain, but
it makes you stop and look and revel in the wonder of it all.
Holy Cross is a fourteener. When you see it you understand
the name. In 1929 Herbert Hoover proclaimed the Holy Cross
area a national monument.

Take I-70 to the Vail Pass rest area. Park in the rest area lot,
and as you come out of the lot turn left and start pedaling up
Shrine Pass Road, Forest Route 709, toward Redcliff. Shrine Pass
Road is a good, wide gravel road. There are a few inviting side
roads along the way. Most are marked as four-wheel-drive and
ATV roads. Shrine Pass Road is very well marked, so don't
worry about getting off and lost unless you want to.

You start out on a 10 percent grade that approaches 20
percent in spots, through a high altitude forest with pine, fir,

and spruce. At the right season, you can expect to see all kinds of wildflowers.

At 1.5 miles you are still climbing a 10-20 percent grade through a subalpine zone. The scenery is great in all directions, from the snowcapped mountains of the Gore Range to the West Tenmile Creek below. The climb turns into a series of easy ups and downs from 1.7 miles to the pass at 2.5 miles. Shrine Pass, elevation 11,089 feet, divides the Arapaho and White River national forests, and Summit and Eagle counties. After the pass it's all downhill to Redcliff.

There is a flat spot at 4 miles with a nice outhouse and an even nicer view of The Mount of the Holy Cross. After a brief respite, head down a relatively steep decline past Lime Creek Road and bear left, staying on Forest Route 709 to Redcliff. The road gets narrower and rougher as you go down, down, down. Be careful with your speed. The Mount of the Holy Cross dominates the forward view.

At 5.5 miles you break out of a thick spruce-fir forest and into a meadow. There is a wall of aspens to the right, on the northwest slope, at around 6 miles. The southeast slope has spruce and subalpine fir. Aspen grow rapidly on sunny sites in areas where other species have difficulty getting a start. As the aspen grow, their own shade inhibits further reproduction because they require direct sunlight. Douglas fir, spruce, and subalpine fir, on the other hand, want a little shade to survive. Over the years, as the soil improves and the aspen provide the umbrella, these conifers replace the aspen. The Dougs, spruce, and fir are climax species. A fire in a climax forest restarts the cycle.

If you have ever had trouble figuring out the difference between Engelmann spruce and subalpine fir, look closely at the mature trees at 7.5 miles. Both are spirelike. Note how gray the fir bark is, and how red-brown the spruce bark is.

On the road again, it's still all downhill. Fun now, but wait till you return. As you descend, the forest changes. Lodgepoles start to show up again. Lower still, the area becomes damp and overgrown. Turkey Creek runs along the now-willow-lined road. At 9.2 miles go past a bridge, continue through a gate at 9.9 miles, and keep rolling up to and over a bridge at 11.8 miles. Enter Redcliff.

Redcliff is a sleepy old mining town named for the quartzite cliffs around it. Silver, gold, copper, lead, and zinc were the economy. Following word of the 1879 Meeker Massacre, locals built a huge log fort. The Utes never made the hundred-plus mile trip down to Redcliff. Back in the 1880s, Redcliff was Eagle County's most important town, with around 800 people, five hotels, two newspapers, and an opera house. Take a few moments to ride around town, maybe grab a bite to eat, fill your water bottle, and head back. The ride back to Shrine Pass is hard. It will take you over twice as long to get back. But . . .you'll feel so good.

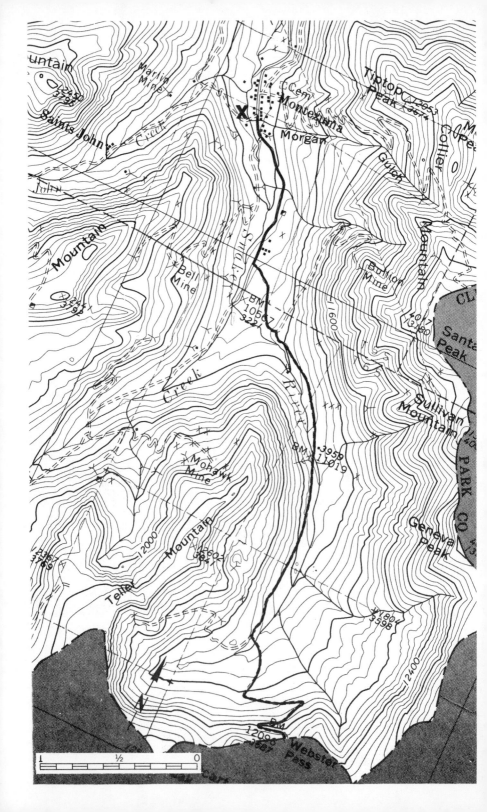

RIDE RATING: Strenuous
SKILL LEVEL: Intermediate
ROUND TRIP: 11 miles
APPROXIMATE RIDE TIME: 3 hours
STARTING ELEVATION: 10,350 feet
HIGHEST POINT: 12,096 feet
MAPS: Arapaho National Forest
       USGS 7.5 Minute Montezuma

12,096

10,350
ROUND TRIP   11

This ride takes you to where the clouds don't float overhead—
they pass by. Webster Pass is above timberline and on the continental divide. Once called Handcart Pass, it was renamed by
the Webster brothers when they built a toll road over it to
serve the Montezuma area mines.

Take U.S. Hwy. 6 to Keystone. Find Montezuma Road on
the east end of Keystone and turn south. If you are coming
from Loveland Pass that's a left. Almost immediately veer to the
left, past a parking area for the ski hill, and continue 5 miles or
so to the town of Montezuma.

Montezuma is an old silver-mining town located on the
Snake River; it really was named after you know who. In 1863
John Coley discovered silver—the first Colorado find. The rush
was on. Montezuma was founded in 1865, and by 1890 it had
over 700 people, two stores, a post office, two hotels, and a
sawmill.

Park in Montezuma and pedal south out of town, on
Montezuma Road, 1 mile to Webster Pass Road. Montezuma
Road is gentle and all-weather gravel. Turn left on Webster Pass
Road; it's marked. Don't turn back when you see the hill. It is
steep and rocky, but it's not that long.

After less than 2 miles you'll come to a national forest sign board. Get in the habit of checking these when you see them. On a July ride, I noted that Handcart Road and Radical Hill Road where both blocked by snow.

Webster Pass Road is a rocky four-wheel-drive road. In general, expect to climb 10-20 percent grades the entire trip up to Webster Pass.

After 2 miles there is a big beaver pond to the right. If you are taking a midsummer tour, you will be treated to columbines, yellow paintbrush, and more. As you might expect at this elevation, the predominant trees are subalpine fir and Engelmann spruce.

There is a nice open area with 360-degree views at about 2.5 miles. The Snake River flows over the road at this point. In July the water was knee high and cold. If you pick your way through the shallow spots, you can ride it and almost stay dry. After the crossing you are confronted with a 20-30 percent incline as you approach timberline.

Being above the trees makes me feel very free yet very vulnerable. I am free to come, but only on nature's terms. Just like the tiny alpine flowers, I must adapt. I love the tundra. Only the unaware think it is barren.

It's a pretty constant 20 percent climb at 3.5 miles. At 3.8 miles there is a fork in the road. To the right is Radical Hill and Deer Creek. To the left is Webster Pass. Go left and climb the final 1.75 miles to the pass. The road has a lot of switchbacks. It is steep. It has a lot of loose stones on it. The ride is arduous but worth every calorie.

There are normally some four-wheel-drive vehicles and ATVs on this road. I did not find them bothersome until I saw a couple of them cut a switchback and drive over the tundra. If you want to avoid traffic, start early.

Webster Pass is at 12,400 feet. There is a great South Park view. While looking at South Park, Red Cone is the red mountain to your left, and Handcart Peak is to your right. If you are lucky you'll see kings crown, alpine buttercup, alpine sunflower, alpine forget-me-not, alpine flock, showy daisy, and sky pilot.

If the road is not blocked by snow, you can take Handcart Road down off the pass and continue all the way to U.S. Hwy. 285. However, don't count on it. For this tour it's back the way we came.

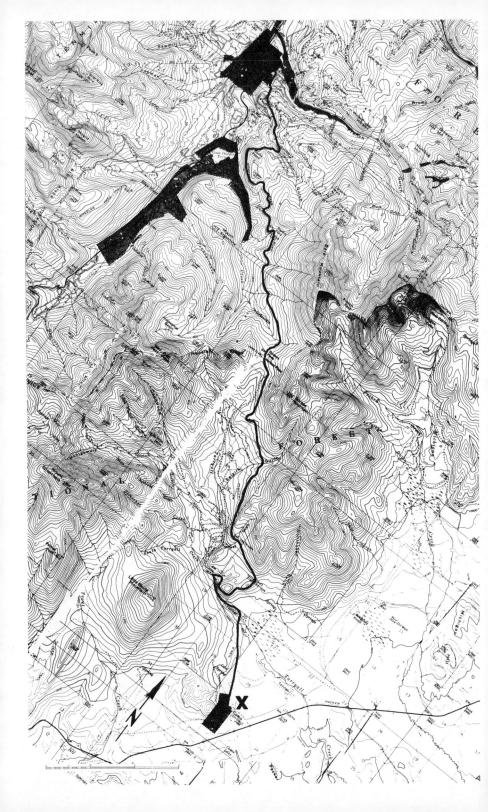

X

Como to Breckenridge **11**

RIDE RATING: Moderate
SKILL LEVEL: Beginning/Intermediate
ONE WAY: 21 miles
APPROXIMATE RIDE TIME: 2.5 hours
STARTING ELEVATION: 9800 feet
HIGHEST POINT: 11,481 feet
MAPS: Pike National Forest, Arapaho National Forest
      USGS 7.5 Minute Como, Boreas Pass, Breckenridge

11,481

9600
ONE WAY   21

Como to Breckenridge takes you over Boreas Bass on Boreas
Pass Road. Once called Breckenridge Pass, Boreas Pass is aptly
named after the Greek god of the north wind. Boreas Pass
Road is the old trackbed for the Denver, South Park and Pacific
narrow-gauge railroad, in its day the highest rail line in the
country. The Army Corps of Engineers rebuilt the route as a
highway in 1937.

Como, named for Lake Como in Italy, was home to the
Italian miners who worked the area. Como was a booming
coal mine and railroad town. You can still see the old
roundhouse.

We all know Breckenridge as an old gold-mining town
yesterday and a good resort and ski town today. The town is
named for U.S. vice-president Breckinridge whose Confederate
sympathies caused incensed locals to change the "i" in the
original name to "e." So much for politics and history.

From Denver take U.S. Hwy. 285 past Bailey, over Kenosha
Pass, and past Jefferson to Como. The Como turnoff, Park
County 50, is roughly 6 miles from Jefferson. Turn right and
proceed into town. Although you can park in Como and pedal
to Breckenridge and then return, this is a good ride to shuttle a
car on. This route description is written as a one-way trip from
Como to Breckenridge.

Ride north, out of town, toward Boreas Pass on Park County 50, an easy gravel road. Proceed past a huge gold dredge dump at 2 miles along the Tarryall Creek. Placer gold, gold found in gravel, is mined by dredging. These goldboat dredges have left huge piles of tailings throughout the area.

At 2.5 miles you'll see the sign for Boreas Pass Road. Turn right and head up a moderate 10 percent grade. Boreas Pass Road is a pretty good dirt road. You are in for some panoramic views as you climb this relatively constant grade. Boreas Pass Road follows North Tarryall Creek.

There is a parking area at 5 miles. If you are looking for a shorter ride, and you do not want to shuttle cars, this is a good place to park and start. From here the grade gets a little more severe, but only for a hundred yards or so.

Selkirk Campground is at 6.8 miles. Gradually the aspen and lodgepole are replaced by spruce and fir. Harebells, fireweed, larkspur, Indian paintbrush, sunflowers, yarrow, and showy daisies are all along the way. As you approach 9 miles, you break out into the open. You'll probably discover why the pass was named after Boreas. Mounts Bross, Democrat, Cameron, and Lincoln outline the divide to the west.

The road gets rockier and steeper as you approach the pass. At 10 miles the krummholz start to appear—those wind-blown trees that get smaller as you get closer to the alpine zone. The road flattens out and switches back less. Alpine sunflowers, buttercups, and elephanthead like this open area.

In another mile you're on the pass at 11,481 feet. Glorious Boreas, from this pass you see the spectacular Ten Mile Range stretching from Quandary Peak to the Gore Range. This is the abandoned town site of Boreas. The old buildings are railroad relics. Here is where you want to eat your lunch.

The ride down the divide and into Breckenridge is fast. The road is in good shape. The views continue. If you have not already done so, you might like to ski this return route in a few months or so.

Bakers Tank, an old DSP&P Railroad steam engine water tank, is at 15 miles. The sign says that of the 64 miles of track from Como to Leadville, the straightest stretch was only 1.6 miles long.

Beyond the tank the descent remains safe and easy as long as you watch your speed. Expect some traffic. After 18 miles you come to the Boreas Pass Winter Trailhead and then pavement. Take the paved road into Breckenridge and find your car.

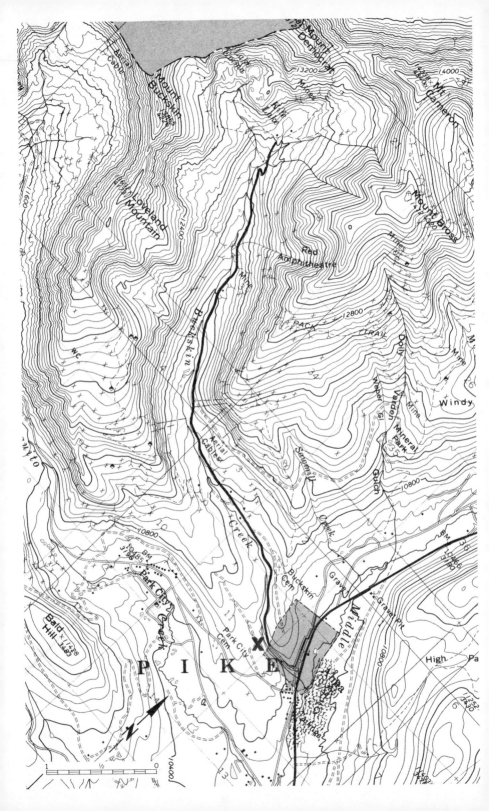

Kite Lake 12

RIDE RATING: Moderate/Strenuous
SKILL LEVEL: Intermediate
ROUND TRIP: 13 miles
APPROXIMATE RIDE TIME: 2 hours
STARTING ELEVATION: 10,353 feet
HIGHEST POINT: 12,000 feet
MAPS: Pike National Forest
        USGS 7.5 Minute Alma, Climax

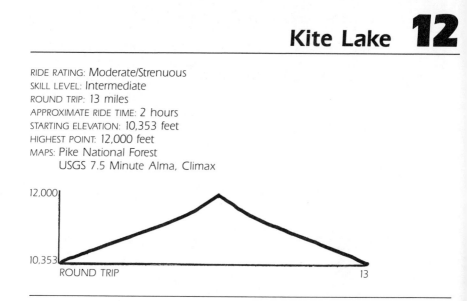

The road from Alma to Kite Lake takes you through real mining country and to the trailhead for climbs up Democrat, Cameron, Lincoln, and Bross; all fourteeners. You can fish and camp at Kite Lake.

The names and the remains of these old gold and silver mines set my mind adrift. It's 1900 and I'm leading an ore-packed burro down the mountain. Why were these mines named Buckskin Joe, Orphan Boy, Hungry Five, Sweet Home, Paris, and Dolly Varden? Close your eyes and find out. This ride starts in Alma, a namesake claimed by three different ladies.

From Fairplay, drive north on Colorado Hwy. 9 for 5 miles to Alma. As you approach the center of town there is a four-way intersection and a gas station. Forest Route 416 is to the west, a left turn if you are coming from Fairplay. Take it, park, and pedal out of town along Buckskin Creek on 416, an all-weather gravel road.

Old mines and abandoned buildings persist. Wildflowers spruce up the rubble. At 3 miles a sign reads "Kite Lake 3 miles." Stay left and continue toward Kite Lake. The road quickly gets rocky and somewhat steep. There are 10-20 percent inclines all along this section. You are up over 11,000 feet and into a spruce-fir ecosystem. Keep an eye out for mule deer.

At 5 miles krummholz stand as monuments to the harsh life on the treeline. The road is rough—a real four-wheel-drive road from here to Kite Lake. At about 6 miles the campground and lake are in view. Getting from here to there is not without some complication. Plan on getting a little wet as you cross the creek that crosses the road that leads to the lake.

Kite Lake is at 5.5 miles. If you decide to park your bike and follow the path up the mountain, you will see the reason for the name Kite Lake. Given seasonable timing, you can eat your gorp amidst the wildflowers. Expect rain in summer and snow in fall.

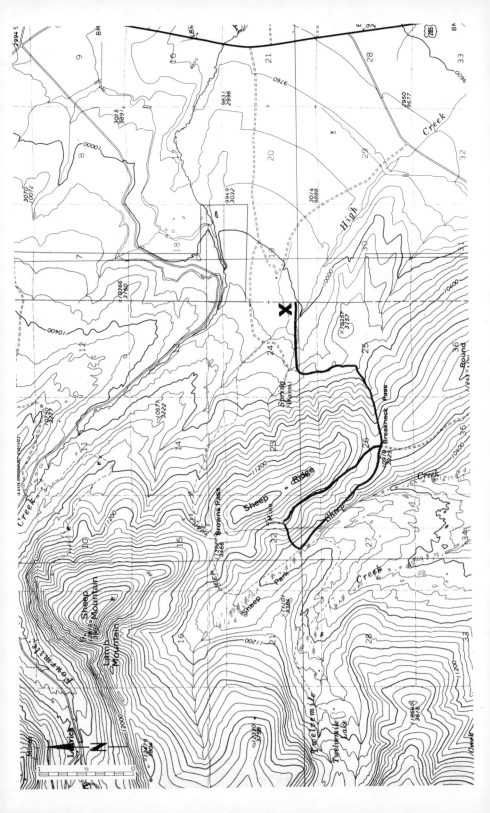

RIDE RATING: Moderate/Strenuous
SKILL LEVEL: Intermediate
ROUND TRIP: 8 miles
APPROXIMATE RIDE TIME: 1.5 hours
STARTING ELEVATION: 10,000 feet
HIGHEST POINT: 11,250 feet
MAPS: Pike National Forest
    USGS 7.5 Minute Fairplay West

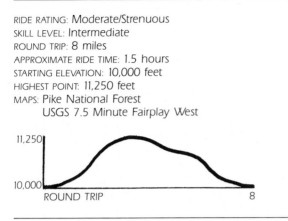

Don't let the name fool you; it's not indicative of the ride. Breakneck Pass is a below-timberline pass between Sheep Ridge and Round Hill, south of Fairplay. Neither the Pike National Forest map nor the USGS Fairplay West quad accurately show this route. Use this book or an updated map.

So many Colorado place names are so unpretentious, colorful, and fun. Researching a name like Fairplay is like going on an historical treasure hunt; one piece of information leads to another. Disgruntled gold seekers were responsible for "Fairplay."

From Fairplay, take U.S. Hwy. 285 south less than 1.5 miles to Weston Pass Road, Park County 5. Turn right and continue about 1 mile to Breakneck Pass Road. Turn right onto Breakneck Pass Road, drive a short distance, and enter the Pike National Forest. If you were feeling strong you could have left your car in Fairplay and pedaled to this point. If you are here with four wheels, park along Breakneck Pass Road, switch to two, and continue into the forest on Breakneck. The data at the top of this route description is for the ride starting at this point on Breakneck Road.

Breakneck is a dirt road. It can get slick when a bit wet, and sloppy when very wet. The first part of the ride is up; not bad, just a modest incline through the aspens. There are good views along the way. Enjoy them now because at 1.2 miles

there is a rocky 40 percent-plus incline, and at 1.7 miles you are still on a 30 percenter. The road levels out around 1.9 miles. There is an intersection at this point. This is Breakneck Pass (10,910 feet). No grand continental divide view, just an intersection amid the lodgepoles.

At the pass turn right on Forest Route 426. Now the mountain views come as you make an easy descent down this jeep road. After 3 miles there is a road to the left, a rocky 20 percent decline. Straight ahead is an old mine, complete with an outhouse with a view. Take the rocky road to the left. Be careful. There is loose rubble all over the road all the way down.

You pop out of the trees and into Sheep Park, an open area at 3.9 miles. The road becomes a two-path dirt road. At 4 miles the road joins another jeep road; turn left. Continue straight ahead at 4.2 miles; don't take the side road over Sheep Creek. Head up the slight incline along the creek. At 5.7 miles you are back at Breakneck Pass. Go back the way you came and enjoy the South Park vista.

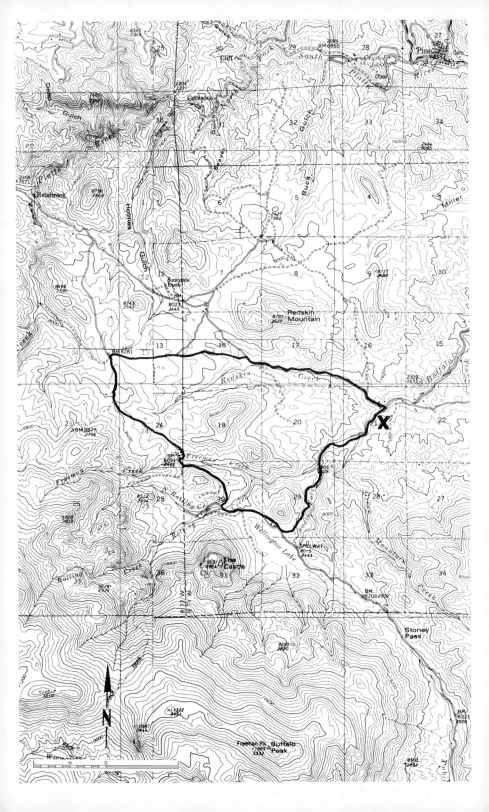

Wellington Lake Loop 14

RIDE RATING: Easy
SKILL LEVEL: Beginning
ROUND TRIP: 12.5 miles
APPROXIMATE RIDE TIME: 2 hours
STARTING ELEVATION: 7300 feet
HIGHEST POINT: 8400 feet
MAPS: Pike National Forest
   USGS 7.5 Minute Green Mountain, Windy Peak

This is a good tour for beginners, families, or more advanced riders looking for a Sunday ride in the park. The ride is on a wide, all-weather gravel road the entire route. A strong mountain bicyclist can cut the ride time in half. If you walk some of the hills you can add an hour. There are enough alternate routes to keep you pedaling all day.

From Denver take U.S. Hwy. 285 south to Pine Junction. Turn left on Pine Valley Road, State Hwy. 126, and proceed 9.5 miles through Pine to Buffalo Creek. Pine and Buffalo Creek are on the old route of former territorial governor John Evans's Denver, South Park and Pacific Railroad. This stretch is part of the North Fork Historic District, and despite three fires in Buffalo Creek, many late nineteenth-century buildings have been preserved.

As you enter Buffalo Creek, look for the Buffalo Creek Recreation Area on the right side of the road; this is the place. You can tack on an extra 12 miles by parking at this point, either along the road or in the Forest Service lot across the highway. Or you can drive roughly 6 miles into the recreation area to the Redskin Group Campground. Park on the roadside or in one of the parking lots in the vicinity.

Pedal southwest along Buffalo Creek on Forest Route 543 toward Wellington Lake. Buffalo Creek flows from Wellington

Lake to the north fork of the South Platte River. It produces some rainbow and brook trout. Lodgepole pine, Douglas fir, and a sprinkling of aspen enclose the road. In summer, columbines, shooting stars, bluebells, Indian paintbrush, and sweet clover color the roadside. Remember this place when it's time to make rose hip jelly.

In about 1.5 miles, as you approach the Green Mountain picnic area, the road climbs at 20 percent for a mile until you reach the overlook at Wellington Lake. This is a fairly strenuous climb if you haven't done this before. The road is in good shape, and this is not a technical climb. Don't give up; go for it. For a fee you can fish, boat, and camp at Wellington Lake. That craggy mountain to the west is The Castle.

Climb Forest Route 543 along the north shore of Wellington another 2 miles to Windy Peak—a Jefferson County outdoor education lab and wildlife refuge. Soon you'll see a nice stand of thinned lodgepoles. This maintenance encourages fat, healthy trees and allows the next generation of trees to get a start beneath the lodgepole boughs. Note the small aspens beneath the pines.

At 7.5 miles from the start, Forest Route 543 intersects the Colorado Trail—a roughly 500-mile Denver to Durango hike. This trail commemorates Colorado's centennial.

In less than another mile you'll catch a glimpse of the continental divide. Shortly after this point you reach the intersection of Forest Route 543 and 550. As an alternate you can ride an easy 8 miles into Bailey. Otherwise, head east on 550 for a 4.5-mile easy downhill run back to the start.

Forest Route 550 is generally traffic free. But, the Wellington Lake area is relatively well traveled. Expect some traffic—not a lot, just some.

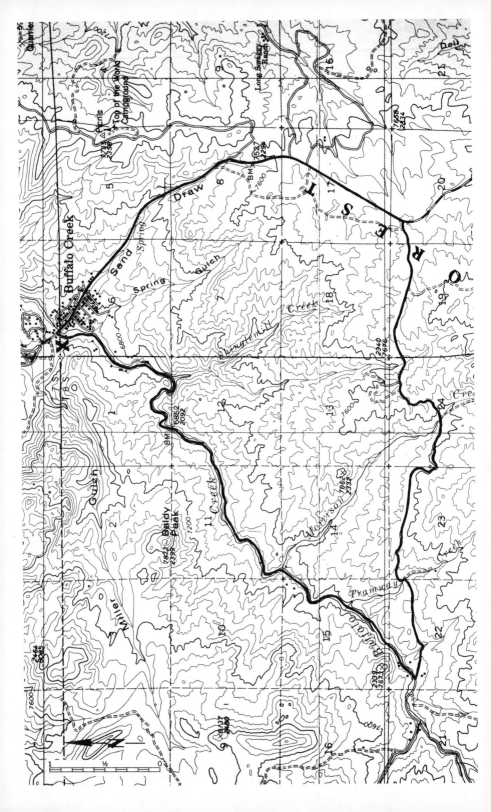

Buffalo Creek Loop **15**

RIDE RATING: Moderate
SKILL LEVEL: Beginning
ROUND TRIP: 14.5 miles
APPROXIMATE RIDE TIME: 2 hours
STARTING ELEVATION: 6680 feet
HIGHEST POINT: 7840 feet
MAPS: Pike National Forest
      USGS 7.5 Minute Pine, Green Mountain, Deckers

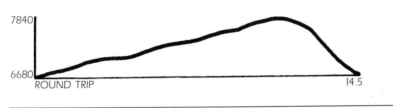

If you have just finished the Wellington Lake loop and are feeling frisky, give this one a try. The Buffalo Creek loop is a little harder than Wellington, but not bad.

If you are just starting, take U.S. Hwy. 285 south to Pine Junction. Turn left on Pine Valley Road, State Hwy. 126, and proceed 9.5 miles through Pine to the town of Buffalo Creek. On the right side of the road, as you enter Buffalo Creek, there is a sign for the Buffalo Creek Recreation Area. Park along the road or in the Forest Service lot across the highway and pedal in to the recreation area on Forest Route 543.

Route 543 is a relatively flat all-weather gravel road. Actually, you will be climbing a very modest incline, but you'll hardly know it. There are several Pike National Forest picnic grounds along 543 starting in a mile at Spring Gulch. Ponderosas are the predominant tree, and the wildflowers come and go early.

There are a few private residences in the area. Buffalo Creek, the creek, runs along 543; if you strapped your fishing pole on your rack, now is the time to break it out. Buffalo Creek is said to harbor a few rainbow and brook trout.

The first 5.5 miles are easy. The road is consistently good. The scenery is pleasant. At close to 6 miles you will come to the intersection of forest routes 543 and 550. Take 550 to the left toward State Hwy. 126. You will quickly come to the Buffalo Campgound.

Hwy. 126 is a winding, sometimes rough, gravel road. For the next 2.5 miles you will be on a roller coaster of relatively modest ups and downs. After a total of 8 miles, you cross Morrison Creek where a primitive road crosses 550. Stay on 550, the main road, and start a fairly strenuous series of 10-20 percent climbs to 7800 feet.

After 10 miles you'll hit State Hwy. 126. Turn left and head north and down the four miles to your car. Hwy. 126 is paved, well traveled, and fast—be careful. When you hit Buffalo Creek take a moment to look around this part of the North Fork Historic District.

Rides in Zone 3

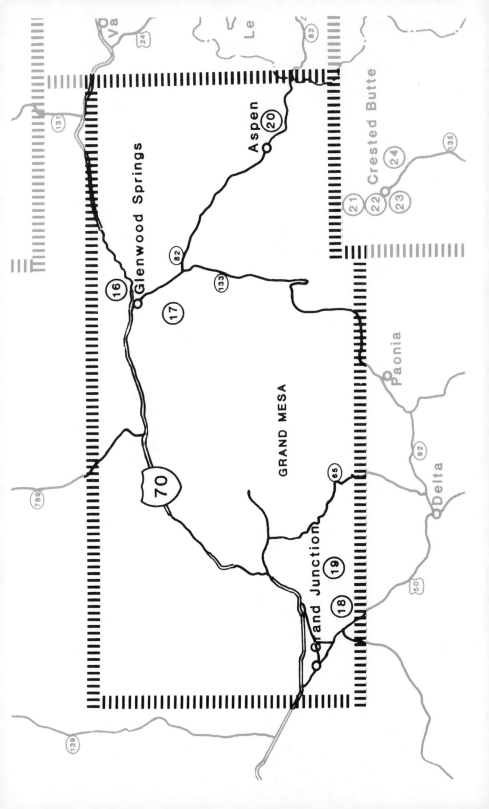

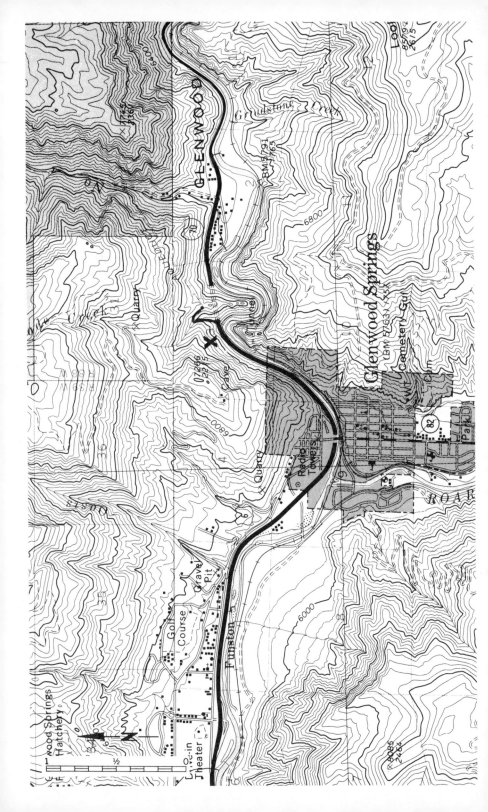

Glenwood Springs Canyon Tanks **16**

RIDE RATING: Strenuous
SKILL LEVEL: Advanced
ROUND TRIP: 4 miles
APPROXIMATE RIDE TIME: 1 hour
STARTING ELEVATION: 5800 feet
HIGHEST POINT: 6200 feet
MAPS: White River National Forest
     USGS 7.5 Minute Glenwood Springs

This is a test. If you are messing around Glenwood Springs itching to test your skill on some steep hills, try this one. This ride starts from the Glenwood Springs hot springs and pool on the north side of I-70 just off the Glenwood Springs exit. Either pedal over to or park at this starting point and head east on Sixth Street, along I-70, toward Glenwood Canyon. Don't let the gate and dead end sign scare you; the road is open to bicycles, it's in good shape, and it's flat.

After about 1 mile there is a pedestrian bridge that crosses over I-70 and leads to a nice and easy ride along the Colorado River on an old closed paved road. Save this one for later. Instead, proceed straight ahead and up a rocky 20 percent grade. This rough road leads to the Glenwood Springs Canyon Tanks. The city of Glenwood Springs collects untreated water from No Name Creek and Grizzly Creek and stores it in these tanks, where it is held for later treatment.

I have listed the White River National Forest Map as a reference, but this road is not on it. It is shown on the referenced USGS quad.

This is a pinon pine-juniper woodland ecosystem. Willow, cedar, and Gambel oak are also in the area. Pinon pine and juniper commonly grow on the same site; thus they are referred to in the same breath, pinon-juniper.

There is some old mining equipment and a waterfall at 1.7 miles followed by a fork in the road. Both forks will take you to the top. If you head left you can do it in style on a rocky 40 percent climb. Remember to lean forward and hunch down over your handlebars. The hardest part is over after 50 yards or so. I went back and tried it again; it's good practice.

The fork you didn't take joins the road at this point. Continue climbing until you reach the water storage tanks at around 2 miles. Water tanks are not real scenic, so just turn around and head back the way you came. For better stability, think about lowering your seat for the steep return. Hikers and spelunkers occasionally use this road, so please be considerate and careful.

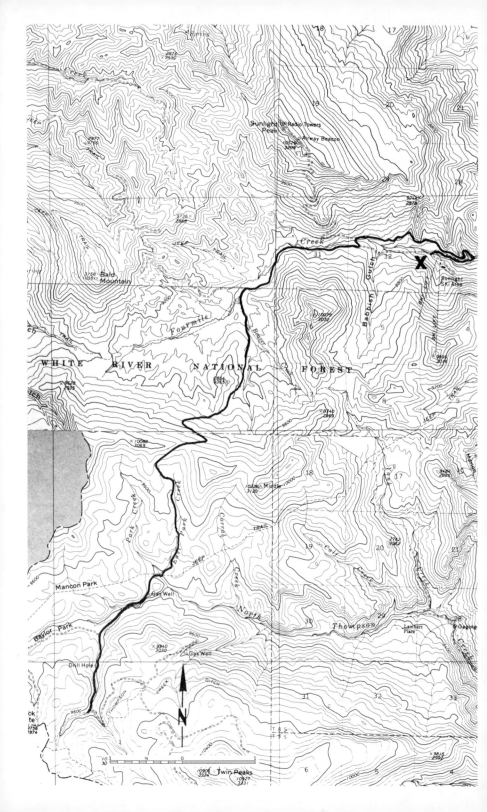

Sunlight to Baylor Park **17**

RIDE RATING: Easy
SKILL LEVEL: Beginning
ROUND TRIP: 26 miles
APPROXIMATE RIDE TIME: 3.5 hours
STARTING ELEVATION: 8100 feet
HIGHEST POINT: 9800 feet
MAPS: White River National Forest
    USGS 7.5 Minute Cattle Creek, Center Mountain, Quaker Mesa

Starting at the Sunlight Ski Area south of Glenwood Springs, this is one of those high-country rides without the hills. This is a good route for beginners, yet with enough miles to give stronger riders a workout. If you are fast, expect to cut an hour off the ride time.

From Glenwood Springs, take Colorado Hwy. 82 south toward Aspen. Follow the signs for the Sunlight Ski Area. South of the main downtown area turn right onto Grand Avenue. Continue about a quarter mile and make another right turn, cross the bridge over the Roaring Fork River, and proceed on 117. In less than another mile there is a fork in the road; keep to the right. Just keep following the ski area signs. After you pass by the Sunlight Mine, you will see the ski area to the left. Take the well-marked left fork that leads to the ski area, park, and unload.

Pedal your bike back to the fork in the road. This time go the other direction—turn left onto Forest Route 300 and head toward Four Mile Park and into the White River National Forest. The road is good, wide, and all-weather gravel. The road is not flat, but the 5 percent incline is not difficult. There are several side roads along the way. Don't be afraid to explore—just remember where the main road is; it is pretty obvious.

I love big aspens, and this area is full of them. At lower elevations in July the wildflowers had had their day, but those

85

big green trunks and silver-green leaves made up for it. Quaking aspen frequently form dense stands as they sprout from the roots of existing trees. Think about this ride in the fall.

At 3 miles you enter the White River National Forest. The ride is still a moderate climb. At 4.5 miles there is an easy downhill run. On a late July tour you will start to see wildflowers. Subalpine fir and Engelmann spruce are now found with the aspen. In time the conifers will crowd out the aspen and become the climax species.

At 5.3 miles the terrain is flat, the road is good, and the view is pleasant—not spectacular, but nice. Climb a 10-15 percent incline at 7 miles, continue through a cattle guard and down again. There is a Forest Service gate and some metal buildings at 10.7 miles. Ride through the gate, past the buildings, and along a small creek until you reach the sign for Haystack Gate and Upper Baylor Park at 12 miles. The road to Upper Baylor Park is a four-wheel-drive road to the left. The road to Haystack Gate is Forest Route 300, the main road—take it to the left.

At 13 miles there is a sign for Haystack Gate to the right and Thompson Creek to the left. This is a good place to reverse direction and head back. However, there are a bunch of roads in the area just waiting to be explored. I end here. Where you end is up to you.

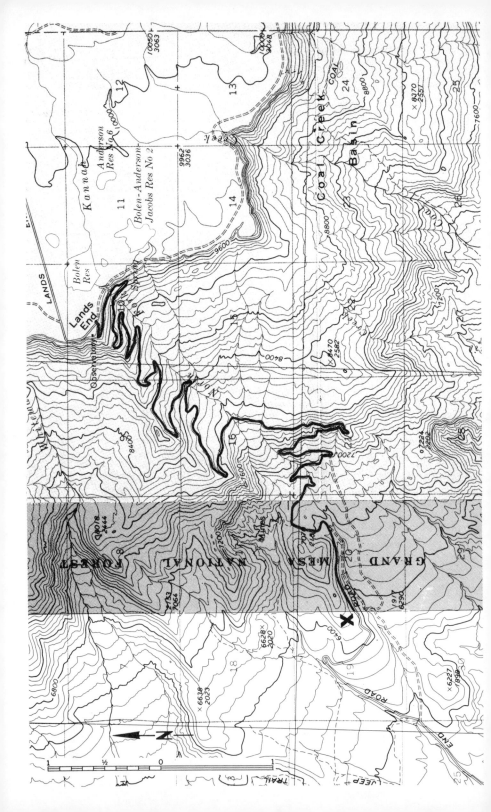

RIDE RATING: Moderate/Strenuous
SKILL LEVEL: Beginning/Intermediate
ROUND TRIP: 24 miles
APPROXIMATE RIDE TIME: 3.5 hours
STARTING ELEVATION: 6500 feet
HIGHEST POINT: 9800 feet
MAPS: Grand Mesa National Forest
    USGS 7.5 Minute Juniata Reservoir, Indian Point, Lands End

This is a ride up and then down Grand Mesa. Billed as one of
the world's highest flattop mountains, Grand Mesa rises to
11,234 feet with roughly an 800-square-mile summit. The mesa
rises above the confluence of the Colorado and Gunnison
rivers. Hence the name Grand Junction. The winter snows that
accumulate on the mesa provide water for the cities and farms
in the valley.

From Grand Junction, take U.S. Hwy. 50 south to Lands
End Road. Lands End Road is about 4 miles south of
Whitewater. Turn east on Lands End Road, continue for 9
miles, and enter the Grand Mesa National Forest. Park along
the side of the forest road. Lands End Road is a good all-
weather gravel road almost all the way to the top. The grades
vary between 5 and 10 percent the entire route. You can't get
lost if you stay on the main road. There is camping along the
way.

At the lower elevations you will see juniper, pinon,
Gambel or scrub oak, and a lot of sagebrush. Juniper and
pinon are seen together, so this area is called a juniper-pinon

89

forest. This juniper-pinon forest is the winter home for a large herd of mule deer.

After less than 1 mile you hit the switchbacks that will take you to the top. Gear down and enjoy the scenery. On the way up you'll catch glimpses of the Colorado National Monument, the Uncompahgre Plateau, the Book Cliffs, and Grand Valley. The valley is wrapped in the red, pink, gray, yellow, and flesh stripes that we use to chart time. There is a lookout at 4 miles. The Book Cliffs and Mount Garfield are to the northwest.

It is estimated that the Colorado River has cut a more than 3000-foot-deep path through the area. The yellow and gray color of the Book Cliffs comes from the shale and clay in the soil. There is almost no vegetation on the cliffs. This is because the clay acts like a sponge, swelling when wet, shrinking when dry. This constant movement makes the soil prone to so much erosion that it cannot support plant growth.

At about 6 miles aspens and wildflowers begin to show up. The road remains much the same. It still goes up, and the surface is still in pretty good shape, even though it does get rougher as you get higher.

The road switches back more frequently as you get closer to the top. The spruce and fir that dominate the top of the mesa now appear along the road. Large rocks form a wall along the road at 10 miles. The road surface remains in good mountain biking shape all the way to the top.

At 12 miles you are at the top. The Lands End Lookout is directly to the left. If you still have some time and energy left you can turn to the Grand Mesa Loop route and tour the top. Otherwise, take a gander at the spectacular view from the Lands End Lookout and head back the way you came. There is traffic on this road, so don't get carried away on the descent.

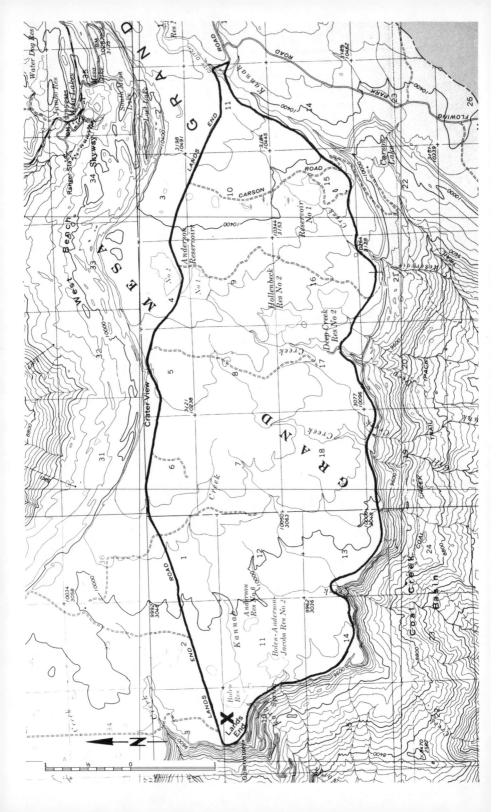

Grand Mesa Loop **19**

RIDE RATING: Easy
SKILL LEVEL: Beginning/Intermediate
ROUND TRIP: 19 miles
APPROXIMATE RIDE TIME: 2 hours
STARTING ELEVATION: 9800 feet
HIGHEST POINT: 10,400 feet
MAPS: Grand Mesa National Forest
      USGS 7.5 Minute Lands End, Skyway

Grand Mesa rises about a mile above the surrounding valley. The Grand Mesa Loop is a flat and easy high-country tour. The colorful cross-valley views are spectacular. The quality of the mesa's fishing holes is well documented. There are several camping areas on top. The summer fields of wildflowers are wonderful. Mule deer, elk, black bear, and many small mammals and birds live on the mesa. I like it.

From Grand Junction, take U.S. Hwy. 50 south to Lands End Road. Lands End Road is about 4 miles south of Whitewater. Turn east on Lands End Road, drive 9 miles to the entrance to the Grand Mesa National Forest, and continue another 12 miles, up the winding road, to the top of the mesa. To the left is Lands End Lookout. You can park in this area.

You can take this loop in either direction—we'll take the southern half first. As of September 1986, the referenced USGS 7.5-minute quads were outdated and did not show this southern part of the loop, the new Lands End Road. The Grand Mesa National Forest map shows it. The old Lands End Road is now called Anderson Road; it is the northern half of this loop.

From the parking area, head south and then east on Lands End Road—no decisions, just follow the road. The road is in good shape. It is a wide all-weather gravel road that hugs the southern edge of the mesa overlooking Coal Creek Basin. The route is generally flat—the gentle inclines along the way can

93

hardly be called hills. The western end of the mesa is open and exposed.

At about 2 miles you will cross Coal Creek. Coal Creek, along with just about every other creek on this side of the mesa, pours down into Kannah, the creek at the bottom of the basin.

On a July ride, the large openings between the trees were filled with a mind-boggling number of wildflowers. I mean large fields of all kinds of them—columbine, Indian paintbrush, yellow paintbrush, scarlet gilia, lupine, penstemon, sunflowers. The stands of Engelmann spruce and subalpine fir pop up more frequently as you move east. Expect to see a marmot or two along the road.

The road conditions are consistently good on this southern section. At around 8 miles you cross Carson Road, Forest Route 108; keep going straight on Lands End. At 10 miles you come to a dirt road marked 105.1. There is a sign for No. 6 Draw along the road. This is Anderson Road. It becomes Forest Route 105. Make a left onto Anderson Road. If you miss this turn you will hit Colorado Hwy. 65 in about 1 mile.

Anderson Road is a rutted dirt road. Be alert. If it's muddy, you are in for some work. Otherwise, if you are a beginner and you take your time, you'll be just fine.

At around 12 miles you pass the other end of Carson Road to the left. Stay on Anderson. Anderson Road runs between Anderson Reservoir No. 1 and No. 2 at about 13 miles. The dirt and ruts continue all along the back stretch. Crater View is at 15 miles; it overlooks the West Bench and the Powderhorn Ski Area. There are a couple of primitive side roads along this stretch; stay on Anderson Road.

After 18 miles you'll come to Bolen Reservoir. Anderson Road curls around the reservoir and then heads back to the Lands End Lookout, and your car.

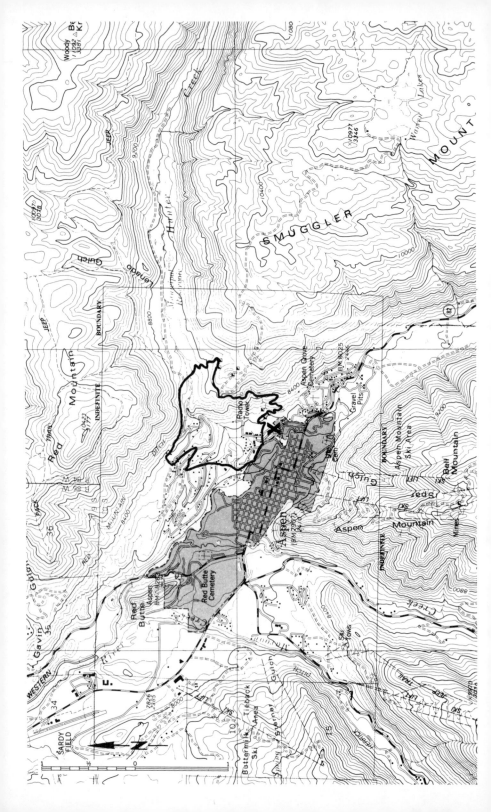

RIDE RATING: Moderate/Strenuous
SKILL LEVEL: Intermediate/Advanced
ROUND TRIP: 8.5 miles
APPROXIMATE RIDE TIME: 2 hours
STARTING ELEVATION: 8100 feet
HIGHEST POINT: 8950 feet
MAPS: White River National Forest
     USGS 7.5 Minute Aspen

8950

8000
ROUND TRIP   8.5

The Aspen area is a great place to ride your mountain bike. There are many good routes in the area. Several are noted in appendix 2, the "other rides" section of this book. The best mountain bike routes in Colorado are in the most beautiful places. For my money Aspen, Telluride, and Crested Butte can't be beat. The Elk, San Miguels, and San Juans are rugged, spectacular mountains. The towns are replete with history, culture, and interest.

When silver was discovered in 1879, the first rush to Aspen was on. Back then Aspen was the largest city on the Western Slope. It had six newspapers. It was considered the most important commercial center between Denver and Salt Lake City. The second rush you know all about.

Smuggler Mountain Road is a good starting place for several different mountain bike rides. To get there, take Colorado Hwy. 82 through Aspen, following it from Main to Original to Cooper, cross over the Roaring Fork River, and turn left on Park Avenue. As Park Avenue bears left, make a right turn onto Park Circle and another right onto Smuggler Mountain Road.

There is a wide area on the right-hand side of Smuggler Mountain Road where you can park and unload. This is a popular route, so expect to see other mountain bikers. The road quickly deteriorates as you climb a 20 percent grade, pass the Smuggler mine, and pedal through a series of switchbacks.

97

Around the turn of the century the Smuggler Mine flooded. Deep-sea divers from New York dove to the pumps, restarted them, and saved the mine. Two days later the pumps stopped again, the divers returned, restarted them again, and then taught a few miners how to be divers.

There are side roads all along the route—no problem though; the main road is pretty obvious. Stay to the right at .5 miles and to the left at 1 mile.

The loose gravel and rocks on the road make it difficult to maintain traction on the 20-30 percent inclines. Many riders will be walking this first part of the tour. Don't despair, soon the ride will become much easier.

Willow, aspen, scrub oak, and sagebrush cover the mountain slope. The summer colors of Indian paintbrush, scarlet gilia, showy daisies, lupine, and sunflowers give way to the brilliant yellow of the aspens in fall. Mount Sopris can be seen to the northwest, while the Elks simply dominate the western landscape.

Turn left at 1.6 miles and head toward Hunter Creek. If you don't go left, and bear to the right, you'll go to the Warren Lakes area, another good ride. At 2 miles stay left and proceed through an aspen-lined flat spot. Then lower your seat and shoot down a steep hill.

At 2.7 miles climb a modest hill and continue into a meadow, where the road soon becomes a two-tread way. Around 3.5 miles you will see a trailhead to the right and a bridge over Hunter Creek straight ahead. Cross over the creek and turn left onto the valley floor and open meadow along Hunter Creek. There are some old abandoned buildings at 4.3 miles built by someone who really knew how to build a room with a view. How about the Maroon Bells?

There is a little loop in the road at 4.5 miles followed by a closed Forest Service gate. Go through, close the gate, and prepare to descend a steep, narrow, and very rocky hill. For the next 100 yards keep your pedals clear of the sides and pick your way through the rocks. Expect to walk.

At 4.9 miles turn right onto a dirt road, continue through a wooden ranch style gate, turn left, and head down the mountain. The gravel turns to pavement at 5.5 miles. Just follow the road down and through a residential area. Now you are in town; watch out for traffic. At 7.5 miles turn left at the Aspen Community Center and head back to your car.

Rides in Zone 4

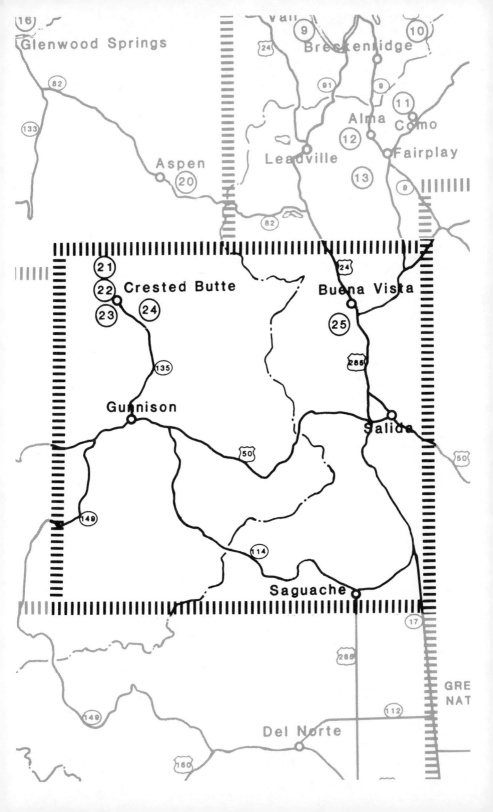

RIDE RATING: Moderate
SKILL LEVEL: Intermediate
ROUND TRIP: 22 miles
APPROXIMATE RIDE TIME: 4 hours
STARTING ELEVATION: 9200 feet
HIGHEST POINT: 10,707 feet
MAPS: Gunnison National Forest
USGS 7.5 minute Gothic, Snowmass Mtn, Oh-Be-Joyful

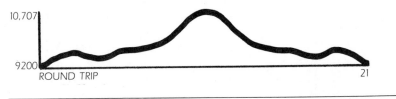

10,707

9200

ROUND TRIP   21

I still get pretty excited when I go from wildflowers to snow.
Mt. Crested Butte to Schofield Pass is that kind of a tour. Drive
north out of Gunnison on Hwy. 135 to Crested Butte, continue
north on 135 for 2 miles to the Mt. Crested Butte ski area. Park
in one of the area lots, pack your lunch, camera, and fly rod,
hop on your mountain bike, and continue north to Gothic.

The first mile of the tour curls through the Mt. Crested
Butte ski village area. With the condos behind you, the pavement soon turns to dirt, and your attention turns to the Elk
Range. The next 4 miles to Gothic are relatively easy, with
rolling terrain and no overall gain in elevation. On a July tour
your senses will be overwhelmed by bursts of color and the
sweet perfume of wildflowers. Scarlet gilia, American vetch,
blue flax, Indian paintbrush, and Colorado columbine are
abundant.

Crossing first the East River and then the bridge over
Copper Creek, you enter Gothic at about 5 miles. A one-time
silver-mining town and one-time ghost town, Gothic is now
home to the Rocky Mountain Biological Laboratory. Gothic was
the most important mining camp in the county. In 1878
Truman Blancett was the first miner in the area. He found six
hundred dollars worth of silver before that winter. Keeping his
find secret, he confided in only two others. When he returned

in the spring, there were about two hundred miners there. By 1880 there were close to a thousand. And so Gothic was founded.

On the north end of Gothic you are confronted with your first steep 30 percent-plus climb, low gear for the hearty, a walk for the not so hearty. The trip from Gothic to Emerald Lake runs along the East River; fair for small brook and rainbow trout. There are a couple of good U.S. Forest Service camp-grounds between 6 and 7 miles out and about 1 mile north of Gothic. They are small, so get there early if you plan to spend the night.

The road is in pretty good shape until about 10 miles, where it turns into a rugged four-wheel-drive road. As you approach Emerald Lake you will hit a few more steep climbs and probably a lot of snow. At one time a large snowbank closed the road for several years. Chances are you will pedal between two walls of snow into the Emerald Lake area. Emerald Lake is full of little trout, and it is said that a big one is occasionally taken.

Continue for less than 1 mile up a rough four-wheel-drive road to 10,707-foot Schofield Pass. If you like you can cross the pass, cycle down through Crystal Canyon, and head into Marble, another 10 miles from the lake. Or you can eat your lunch and go back to Mt. Crested Butte. The ride back to Mt. Crested Butte is fast, cool, and just as scenic from the opposite direction.

Upon your return you may wish to dally around the town of Crested Butte, a turn-of-the-century coal-mining boomtown and national historic district named after the distinctively shaped 12,162-foot mountain to the northeast.

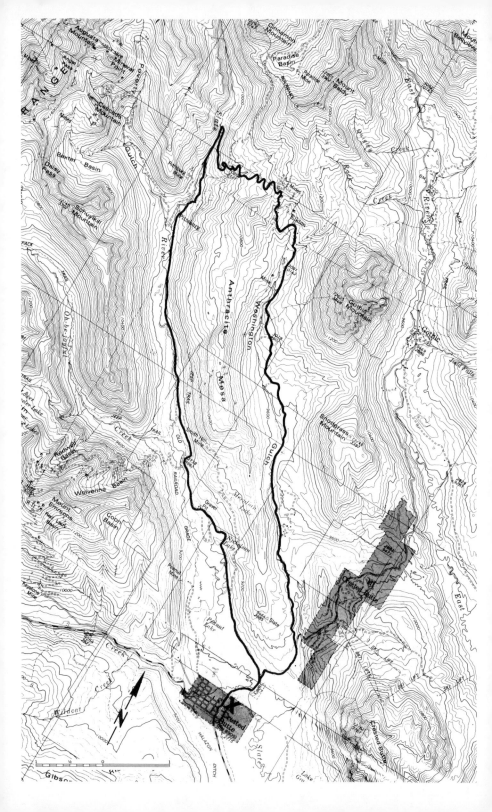

RIDE RATING: Moderate/Strenuous
SKILL LEVEL: Intermediate
ROUND TRIP: 23.5 miles
APPROXIMATE RIDE TIME: 4 hours
STARTING ELEVATION: 8880 feet
HIGHEST POINT: 11,000 feet
MAPS: Gunnison National Forest
USGS 7.5 Minute Crested Butte, Gothic, Oh-Be-Joyful

This is Crested Butte—big time fat tire country. There are probably more documented mountain bike routes in the mountains around Aspen and Crested Butte than in any other area of the state. You can stay for a few days and just bike. What these towns have in common is charm, the Elk Mountains, and old mines. Miners made roads that are now great for mountain biking. Other towns, like Telluride and Montezuma, have similar formulas, but Crested Butte and Aspen have developed it and capitalized on it.

The first part of this tour, say up to Pittsburg, is easy/moderate for a beginner. Beyond Pittsburg it gets pretty strenuous and tricky in places; not dangerous, just tricky. Crested Butte to Pittsburg is a good beginning 16 mile ride.

To get there, take Colorado Hwy. 135 north out of Gunnison to the town of Crested Butte. Hwy. 135 bears to the left as you enter Crested Butte. Just before downtown, and just as 135 turns right and goes up to the ski hill, there is a parking area. Unload and continue on 135 toward the Mt. Crested Butte Ski Area. In less than 1 mile you will see a cemetery on your right and Gunnison County 734 to your left. Turn right onto 734 and proceed along the Slate River toward Pittsburg. Pittsburg is only a sign along the road, but once it was a flourishing gold camp.

At this point the road is a pretty civilized gravel road. The grade is moderate—if you're not in a hurry you won't sweat much. Expect some traffic. Pedal by Nicholson Lake at 3 miles and continue to a fork in the road at 3.5 miles. Stay to the right and on the main road.

Lodgepoles enclose the road at 4 miles as you start a brief descent and a series of ups and downs. Gunsight Pass Road is at 4.7 miles; keep to the right. The road gets steeper as you get higher. The grade is pushing 10 percent at about 5 miles. There is evidence of coal mining in the area. That's Anthracite Mesa to the right. This is the site of the Smith Hill coal mine. Minerals were mined but Crested Butte was a coal town.

Aspen, Engelmann spruce, and subalpine fir replace the lodgepole pine. Think about this route when the aspen turn. The wildflowers on a midsummer ride are also a treat. You'll encounter Oh-Be-Joyful Road at 6 miles. The name says it all.

Continue on this rollercoaster on up to Pittsburg at 8 miles. There are some really nice Elk Mountain views along the way. At 8.5 miles Slate River Road and Poverty Gulch Road are to the left; continue straight ahead on 734 toward Paradise Pass. From here on expect to do some climbing. The grade is about 15 percent at 8.7 miles, 20-30 percent at 8.8 miles, and 40 percent in some places before you get to 9 miles. There are a couple of washed-out areas between here and the top. In August they were easy to cross.

At 10.3 miles make a hard right and start an arduous climb to 10.6 miles. Getting up a hill like this has a lot to do with your state of mind. You can do it. Now, you didn't expect it to be flat at 10.6 did you? It's 20 percent inclines for the next couple of miles.

Forest Route 811.3A is at 12.2 miles; it will take you back down Washington Gulch, where it becomes Gunnison County 811. If you continue on 734 you'll hit Paradise Pass. From there you can pedal over to Schofield Pass. Try it another day. For now, take 811.3A.

Continue a moderate climb to 12.8 miles, bear left on the obvious main road, climb a short 30 percent incline, and continue with a few ups and downs to the top at 13.4 miles.

That's Mt. Crested Butte ahead of you. Gothic and Snodgrass mountains are to the left. There is a nice campsite at the top. The descent is steep, the gravel is loose, and the corners are tight. Your rear wheel will want to skid. Take it easy.

Elkton is at 14 miles. Watch the trees change as you descend from one life zone to another. The road levels off at 17 miles as you ride through a big meadow. This is Washington Gulch.

Signs of modern civilization appear and the road gets better as you approach 19 miles. Descend to Hwy. 135, turn right, and head back down to town.

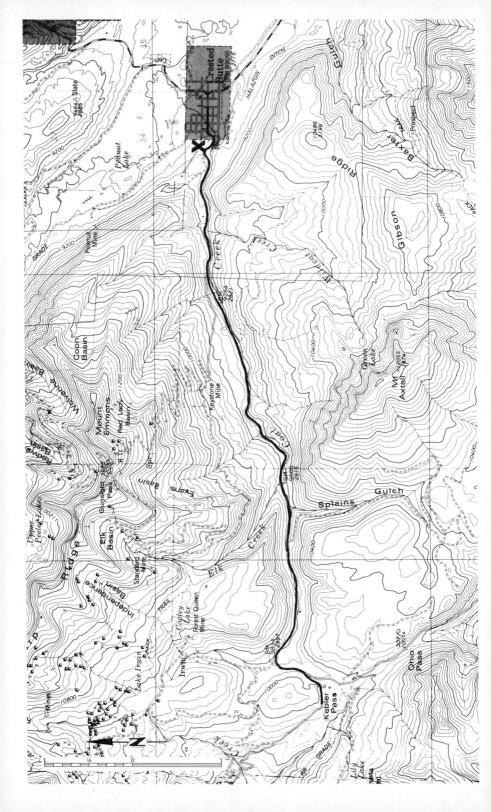

RIDE RATING: Moderate
SKILL LEVEL: Beginning
ROUND TRIP: 15 miles
APPROXIMATE RIDE TIME: 1.5 hours
STARTING ELEVATION: 8880 feet
HIGHEST POINT: 10,007 feet
MAPS: Gunnison National Forest
    USGS 7.5 Minute Crested Butte, Mt. Axtell

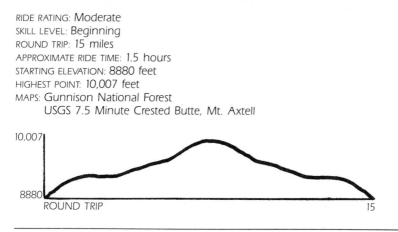

Kebler Pass (10,007 feet) is between Crested Butte and Paonia. This description and heading cover a tour from Crested Butte to the pass and back. Park in Crested Butte and pedal to Gunnison County Hwy. 12 on the southwest end of town; about .5 miles from downtown. Crested Butte is not a very big place; there is only one road heading west out of town—Hwy. 12. Look for the sign "Kebler Pass Open" (you hope), then head west and up a moderate incline.

Hwy. 12 is a good all-weather gravel road with moderate grades and some traffic. The road follows Coal Creek, Crested Butte's water supply, and flows into the Slate River. There is a mingling of aspen, spruce, and fir.

At 2.2 miles follow the sign to Kebler Pass and soon enter the Gunnison National Forest. Continue up a pretty consistent but easy incline. Note the avalanche chute at 4.5 miles. The road runs through a meadow with snowcap views at 6.5 miles. The road to the Lake Irwin Campground is to the right at 6.8 miles. Stay to the left on Kebler Pass Road. At 7.2 miles the road to Ohio Pass, Forest Route 730, is to the left. Ohio Pass is only about 1.5 miles up the road; try it later. We're going to Kebler Pass, so keep right and hit the pass at 7.5 miles. This is not one of our spectacular Colorado mountain passes, but it is a good beginning ride with nice scenery.

If you are looking for a few more miles, you can continue down the other side of the pass toward Paonia. The road remains the same, and the ups and downs are all moderate. There is camping at Horse Ranch Park, 4.8 miles from Kebler Pass.

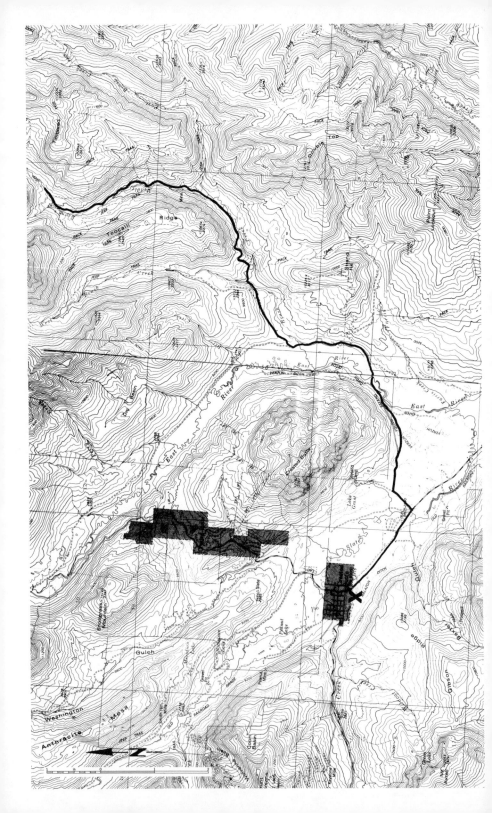

RIDE RATING: Strenuous
SKILL LEVEL: Advanced
ROUND TRIP: 29 miles
APPROXIMATE RIDE TIME: 4.5 hours
STARTING ELEVATION: 8880 feet
HIGHEST POINT: 10,500 feet
MAPS: Gunnison National Forest
    USGS 7.5 Minute Crested Butte, Gothic, Pearl Pass

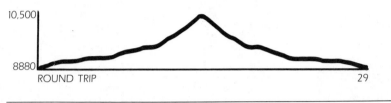

10,500

8880

ROUND TRIP   29

This is a classic mountain bike ride; the grades, rocks, and water make it a challenge. The views and the feeling of accomplishment make it worthwhile.

Assuming that you have left your car in Crested Butte, pedal toward Gunnison on Colorado Hwy. 135, cross the Slate River at about 1.8 miles, and almost immediately turn left onto Forest Route 738 and follow the sign for the airport. Route 738 is a wide gravel road. It winds through the meadow at the base of Crested Butte, past condos, a resort, and a golf course. At 2.8 miles cross a cattle guard and start a moderate climb past the airport at 3 miles. Watch for stock on the road.

Sagebrush, aspen, and, in summer, wildflowers bedeck the land. Expect to see lupine, scarlet gilia, blue flax, potentilla, Indian paintbrush, columbine, and I'm sure many more. Look for bluebirds perched on fence poles.

Cross a creek at 4.7 miles, stay on the main road, cross Brush Creek at 6.6 miles, cross it again right after, and continue to the sign for Brush Creek Road at 6.7 miles. Take Brush Creek Road toward Pearl Pass 12 miles ahead. The route continues on a rutted four-wheel-drive road. The grade is around 10 percent. At 7.1 miles there is a gate; open it, go through it, and close it. Respect private property. There is another gate at 7.2 miles; pass through and enter the Gunnison National Forest at 7.8 miles or

so. There is a fork in the road—follow the sign and go right to Pearl Pass on Brush Creek Road.

There is a dropoff at 8.1 miles—be careful. At about 8.4 miles you'll see West Brush Creek to your right. Don't go straight, cross the creek instead. In midsummer the creek was eighteen inches deep, twenty feet wide, and moving fast. It's a two-part crossing: wade the first and ride the second. You'll come out on a four-wheel-drive road by a campsite. Continue up a 20 percent grade and then climb a roughly 100-yard-long 30 percent incline to a three-way intersection at 8.8 miles. The main road goes left; take it. It's not marked, but it does go to Pearl Pass. The road to the right is marked 409 and the sign says Ferris Creek. The middle fork dead ends.

Don't think that the climbing is over. It's 10 percent changing to 30-40 percent at 9 miles. It is very difficult to keep the front wheel down; time to reread the skills section in the beginning of this book. There is a steep descent at 9.5 miles. The road is rocky and rutted. Cross Middle Brush Creek at 10.9 miles. In August it was eighteen inches deep, twenty-five feet wide, and moving relatively fast.

Intersect East Brush Creek Road at 11.3 miles, but don't take it; stay to the left and continue on Brush Creek Road. The sign says 8 miles to Pearl Pass. Take a break from the climb and look at the big aspens. At 12 miles there is a nice mountain view to the left. At 13 miles there is a waterfall to the right. There are little freshets running over the road all along this section. The road is steep and rocky.

Pedal through a high mountain meadow at 14.2 miles and continue to the Twin Lakes and Pearl Pass sign at 14.5 miles. This is where I turned back. Pearl Pass is straight ahead. Let me tell you about Pearl Pass. The opening of Pearl Pass created a link between two of Colorado's most famous mining towns, Crested Butte and Aspen. The elevation is 12,705 feet. The final 5 miles are demanding; steep and rocky. If you are up for it, expect to take over an hour to get to the pass. If you continue down the other side of the pass you can ride to Ashcroft and then to Aspen. Back on the road at 14.5 miles, lower your seat and hang on for the return trip.

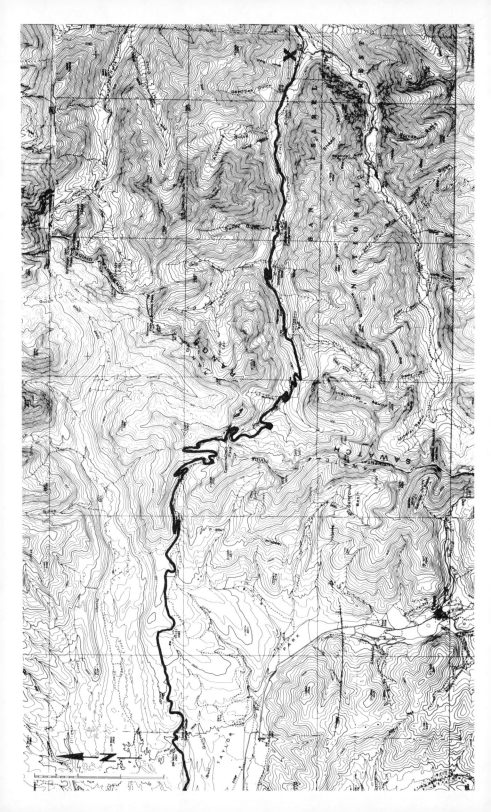

Buena Vista to Taylor Park Reservoir **25**

RIDE RATING: Moderate
SKILL LEVEL: Beginning
ONE WAY: 26 miles
APPROXIMATE RIDE TIME: 3 hours
STARTING ELEVATION: 8400 feet
HIGHEST POINT: 12,126 feet
MAPS: San Isabel National Forest, Gunnison National Forest
    USGS 15 Minute Buena Vista
    USGS 7.5 Minute Mt. Yale, Tincup, Taylor Park Reservoir

This ride takes you over Cottonwood Pass. It is written as a one-way trip. You can decide what you want to do—shuttle a car, go over and back, go part way, whatever. This is a good ride; it doesn't require a lot of skill, but you will work a little. Be sure to check and make sure the pass is open.

To get there take U.S. Hwy. 24 to Buena Vista. Buena Vista is wedged between the Mosquito Range to the east and the Sawatch Range to the west. Both ranges are part of a single uplift and together form a single wide faulted anticline.

Stretching from The Mount of the Holy Cross to Mt. Massive, the Sawatch Range has the largest mountains in the state, including the three highest: Mt. Elbert (14,433 feet), Mt. Massive (14,421 feet), and Mt. Harvard (14,420 feet).

The mountains in the Collegiate Group of the Sawatch Range are conspicuous by their names. Since there is a limited number of Ivy League colleges, several peaks escaped with names like Huron and La Plata.

Back on the road again, follow U.S. Hwy. 24 through Buena Vista to Chaffee County 306. Take 306 west and drive toward Cottonwood Pass. After about 4 miles you will enter the San Isabel National Forest. Continue on 306. At 6.5 miles the road turns to gravel; this is a good place to start.

Prior to the opening of Independence Pass, Cottonwood Pass was the main supply route to the Aspen area mines. Once a toll road, today this road is the primary route between Buena Vista and Taylor Park Reservoir. It is a good road with moderate grades and good views, but with some traffic. The road follows Cottonwood Creek for much of the way.

Start pedaling up a 10 percent incline. Expect 5-10 percent grades the entire ride to the pass. In less than a mile you will pass the Rainbow Lake Resort. Lodgepole start to join the aspen along the road. Aspen and lodgepole pine occasionally grow together; more frequently, one or the other will take over a site. At over 8400 feet this is the montane life zone.

The Collegiate Peaks Campground is at 3.7 miles. After about 4 miles the road levels off, but it also starts to get a little rougher. After a few easy ups and downs you start a constant climb to the top. Along the way note how the fir and spruce start to dominate as you cross into the subalpine life zone. Pass the Ptarmigan Lake Trail Head at 7.5 miles. You're still climbing at 8 miles.

Jones Mountain is to the south at 9 miles. You are at around 11,000 feet and approaching timberline. There are grand mountain views all along as you climb past timberline and hit the pass at 12.5 miles.

Cottonwood Pass is at 12,126 feet. It is the dividing line between the San Isabel and Gunnison national forests. To the north is the Collegiate Peaks Wilderness. To the west is the Elk Range. I didn't see any cottonwoods on top, but on this August day I did see yellow paintbrush, alpine sunflowers, yellow buttercups, Indian paintbrush, and American bistort.

The road to the Taylor Park Reservoir heads down a 10 percent grade. There are some washboard conditions on the road. Be careful—it's easy to mountain gaze and lose it. Timberline Overlook is at 13.5 miles.

At about 16 miles you start to get into the trees again. Stopping to look at the wildflowers we were attacked by mosquitoes. Before a fatal amount of blood was lost we saw fireweed, mountain bluebells, and fringed gentian.

There is a nice meadow and a beaver pond after 18 miles. The road improves as you get lower. The cars can raise some dust, but it's not bad. The trees change in reverse order on the descent. The Taylor Park Ranger Station is at 24.5 miles. From here the free ride is over and you have to pedal again. Taylor Park Reservoir, the end, is at 26 miles.

Rides in Zone 5

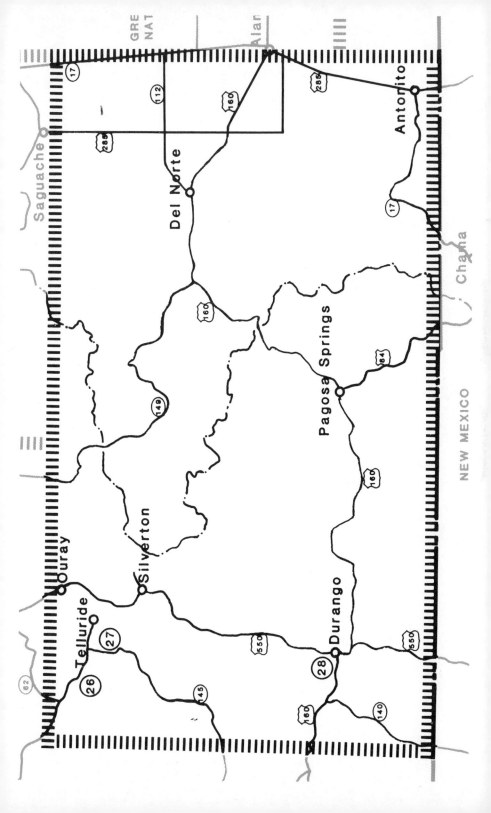

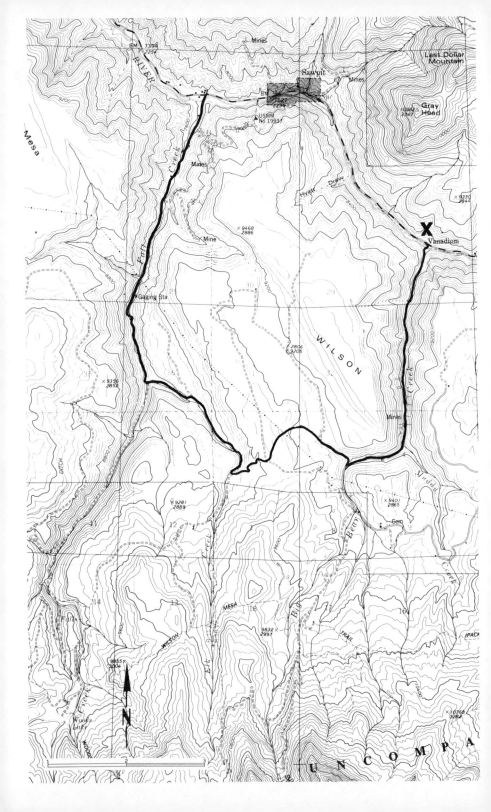

Silver Pick Road/Fall Creek Road

RIDE RATING: Moderate
SKILL LEVEL: Beginning
ONE WAY: 11.5 miles
APPROXIMATE RIDE TIME: 2 hours
STARTING ELEVATION: 8010 feet
HIGHEST POINT: 9200 feet
MAPS: Uncompahgre National Forest
    USGS 7.5 Minute Gray Head

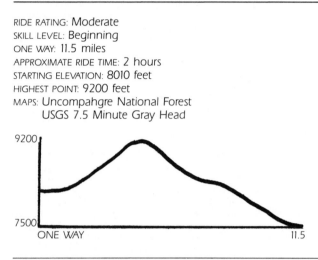

This is one of many good rides around Telluride. Compared to some this one is pretty mellow. You have a few route options. You can shuttle a car from Silver Pick Road to Fall River Road. You can make a grand loop and return to the start on Colorado Hwy. 145. Or you can ride from Silver Pick Road to Hwy. 145 and then just return the way you came. This description covers only the one-way trip from Silver Pick Road up over Wilson Mesa to Hwy. 145. Don't depend on the two maps listed above; neither has been updated to correctly show this route. Use them for an overall look at the area, but use this book for an accurate route description.

Wilson Mesa is named for A. D. Wilson, chief topographer for the Hayden Survey. There's more on Wilson and the survey in the Alta route description.

Take Colorado Hwy. 145 west out of Telluride about 7 miles and turn left on Silver Pick Road, San Miguel County 60.M. You can park in the parking area just off Hwy. 145. Pedal over the bridge and start up a 10 percent incline on a good gravel road along Big Bear Creek.

There is a mixture of aspen, cottonwood, ponderosa pine, blue spruce, Douglas fir, Engelmann spruce, and subalpine fir along the route. At around 3 miles the road starts to get

rougher. There may also be some slick spots if it is wet; be careful. Continue to the fork in the road at 3.3 miles. A left takes you to Silver Pick Basin. Don't go left; go right toward Wilson Mesa on San Miguel County 56.L. It gets a little harder now as part of the climb approaches 20 percent.

At 4 miles, as you approach the top, there is a horse ranch with a view. Once up on the flat mesa top, it's an easy ride. Enter the Wilson Mesa Ranch area at 4.5 miles and continue on 56.L, now a dirt road, down an easy descent to the sign at 5.1 miles. Bear right on 56.L and down toward Elk Creek; stay on 56.L and turn right as the road ends at an unmarked intersection at 5.9 miles. You are still on 56.L.

Stay on the obvious main road and cruise down over a cattle guard at 6.9 miles, over a new bridge at 7.8 miles, and up to the intersection with 57.P. Although it doesn't say so, 57.P is Fall Creek Road. Turn right onto 57.P and begin an easy climb along the creek. The road gets better, not that it was bad, but it gets better.

Cross Fall Creek at 10.8 miles, the San Miguel River at 11.4 miles, and hit the highway at 11.5 miles.

You can return the way you came, you can turn right and take Hwy. 145 back to the start, or you can hop in your car if you shuttled.

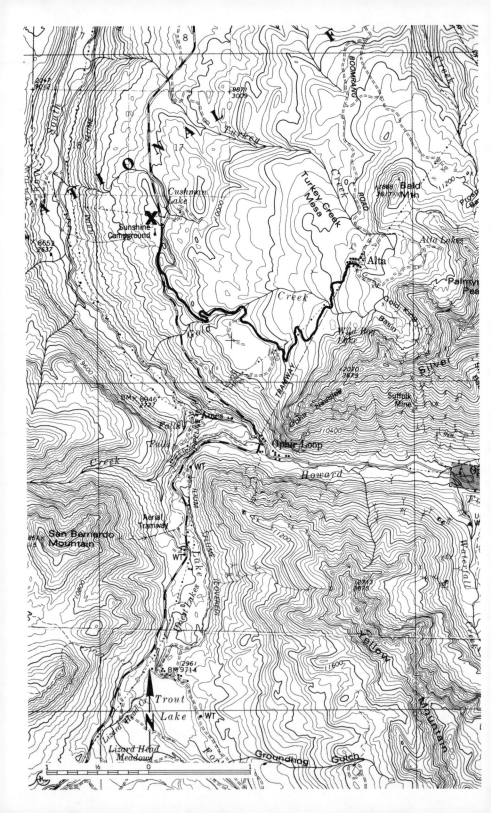

RIDE RATING: Moderate
SKILL LEVEL: Intermediate
ROUND TRIP: 9 miles
APPROXIMATE RIDE TIME: 1.5 hours
STARTING ELEVATION: 9600 feet
HIGHEST POINT: 11,000 feet
MAPS: Uncompahgre National Forest
    USGS 7.5 Minute Gray Head, Telluride, Ophir
    USGS 15 Minute Telluride

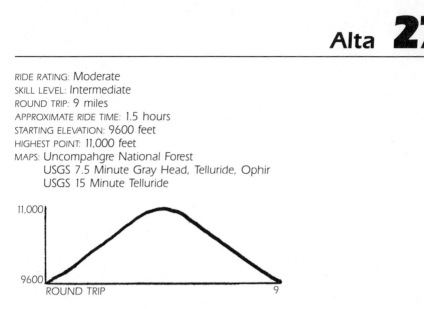

This one is short, but it has dramatic views that are arguably the most spectacular in this book. The San Juan and San Miguel mountains are awesome. To get there take Colorado Hwy. 145 west out of Telluride 3.5 miles to 145 south. Turn left, south, and head toward Dolores. In less than 9 miles from Telluride you'll see the Sunshine Campground on your right. This is a good place to park. Hop on your bike and continue south on 145 for less than 1 mile. Turn left onto Forest Route 632 toward Alta Lakes; it's well marked.

Note that it takes a corner of three USGS 7.5-minute quads to cover this ride. There are not many Colorado 15-minute topo maps in print anymore—there is a 1955 Telluride topo still around. Telluride may have changed, but the mountains haven't. Depending how you plan to use it, this may be a good alternative map.

The road starts out as a narrow, rough road with a moderate incline that quickly becomes a constant 10-15 percent grade. I would have no problem taking my four-wheel- drive truck on it, but I would think twice about the family car.

In August you can see scarlet gilia, showy daisies, sunflowers, harebells, Indian paintbrush, yarrow, and fireweed.

Spruce, fir, and aspen predominate. I spotted a couple of mule deer and a marmot along the way.

Wilson Peak (14,017 feet) and Sunshine Mountain (12,930 feet) are on your right, to the west, as you wind up the hill. I don't have a single mountain named after me, but A. D. Wilson has two; both fourteeners. He also has Wilson Meadows, Wilson Mesa, Wilson Creek, and probably more. A. D. Wilson, chief topographer for the Hayden Survey in 1874, was also a mountain climber of note.

The eight-year Hayden survey was a most extensive exploration of the Rocky Mountains. Ferdinand V. Hayden et al. measured, climbed, photographed, described, and sketched much of Colorado, and then summarized it all in *The Geological Atlas of Colorado and Portions of Adjacent Territory*. This catalog eased the way for the railroad and mining companies.

Back to the road; after 1 mile it's still up. Don't expect any less. The bumps and the 10-15 percent climb will continue all the way to the top. At 2.5 miles there is a good view of jagged Silver Mountain straight ahead. Like a stockade wall, the big, fat, green trunks of the aspen enclose the road in places. Pass a side road at 3.5 miles and continue pedaling through an open meadow. Pass another side road at about 4 miles and come to an intersection of three roads at a little over 4.3 miles. Take the middle road, bear to the left, and hit Alta at about 4.5 miles.

Names like Gold Basin, Silver Mountain, and Gold Creek suggest that this site was selected for reasons other than the view, but I suspect more than one tired miner was awestruck by a setting sun. Alta was a mining camp primarily for the Gold King Mine, which produced gold, silver, lead, and copper. All three of the Alta mills have burned down. Before you head down you might like to explore a bit and continue around the back to Alta Lakes.

The return trip is fast. The road is narrow, and there is likely to be some traffic. Don't get too carried away.

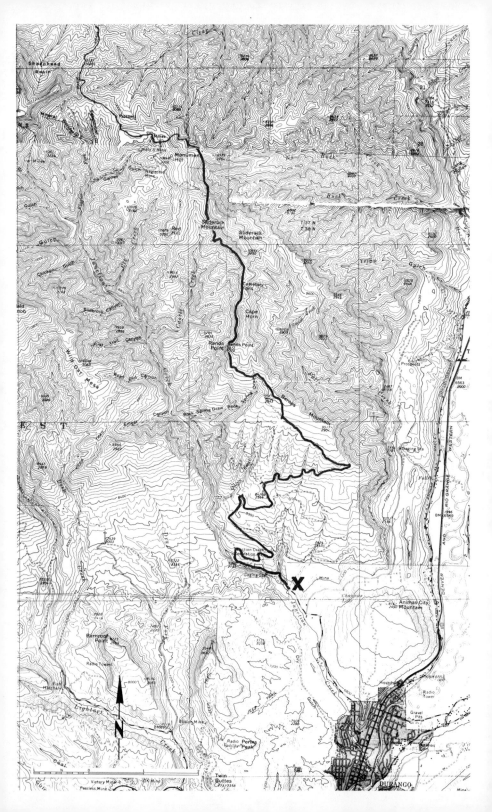

RIDE RATING: Moderate
SKILL LEVEL: Beginning
ROUND TRIP: 37 miles
APPROXIMATE RIDE TIME: 5 hours
STARTING ELEVATION: 7000 feet
HIGHEST POINT: 10,500 feet
MAPS: San Juan National Forest
USGS 7.5 Minute Durango West, Monument Hill

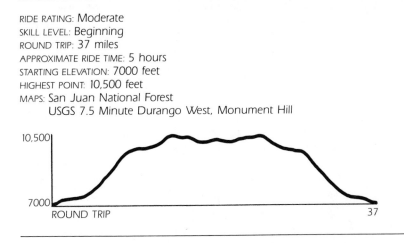

This Monument Hill is north of Durango. In 1880, Durango, which was named after a town in Mexico, which was named after a town in Spain, was intended to be the Denver of Southern Colorado. Cattle, trains, gold and silver, a booming red-light district, shootouts, and free lots for any church that wanted to try its luck are all part of the lore.

From Durango, take U.S. Hwy. 550 north and turn left onto Fifth Street. Fifth Street turns into Junction Street. Drive through a residential area, past the junior high school, and up to a fork in the road at about 2 miles from 550. Bear left and follow the sign to the San Juan National Forest. At about 3.5 miles from 550, cross a cattle guard, enter the national forest, park along the road, hop on your bike, and continue up the road you are on—Junction Creek Road.

Junction Creek Road follows Junction Creek for a while. The road is good. The climb is moderate. The way is lined with Gambel oak, cottonwood, willow, Douglas fir, ponderosa pine, and plenty of wildflowers. Midsummer brings fireweed, harebells, Indian paintbrush, yarrow, gentian, and more.

The Junction Creek Campground is in about 1.5 miles from the national forest entrance. There are good lookouts on both sides all along the road. After pedaling 2 miles or so there is a

Durango overlook. At 4 miles you are still climbing a 10 percent grade on a good road. There is an excellent view of the Animas River Valley at around 7 miles. At this point notice the change in the trees; fewer ponderosa, more spruce and aspen.

After 10 miles you can see the probably snowcapped peaks of the LaPlata (silver in Spanish) Mountains to the west. The route continues over a series of gentle ups and downs all along the ridge. This is a mellow ride. If you are looking at a USGS quad, don't be confused; the road has changed. There is a new road up to and past Monument Hill. You can't miss it; it is the good road. If you stay on it you won't go wrong.

Monument Hill is at about 11.5 miles. There are several old mines in the area. For the next 5 miles there are great views on both sides of the road. The road is a bit narrower now, but it is relatively new and in good shape.

At 18.5 miles there is a three-way junction with Neglected Trail and Clear Creek Trail. This is a good place to turn around and head back.

Rides in Zone 6

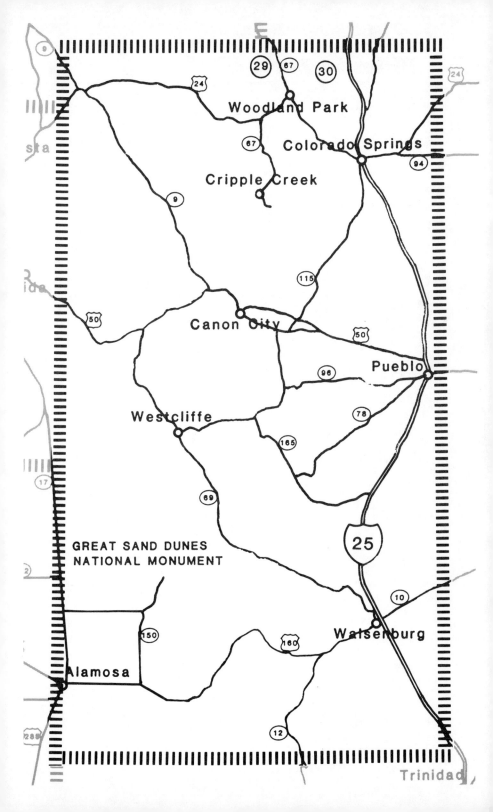

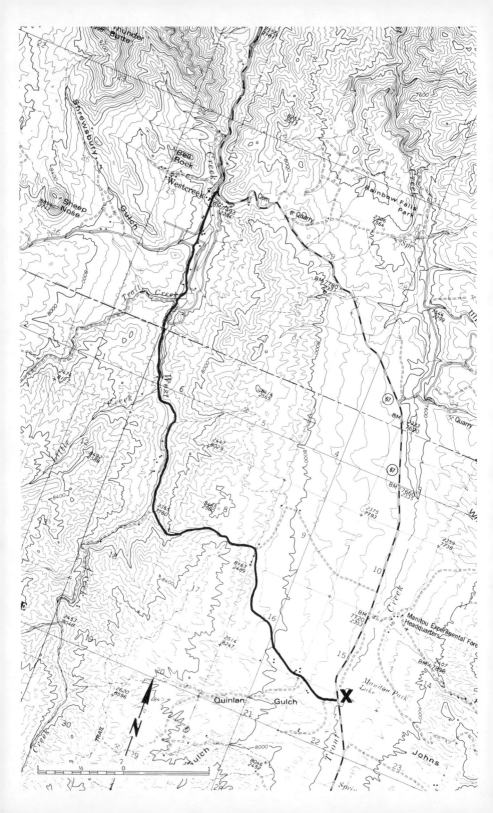

RIDE RATING: Moderate
SKILL LEVEL: Beginning
ONE WAY: 8 miles
APPROXIMATE RIDE TIME: 2 hours
STARTING ELEVATION: 7850 feet
HIGHEST POINT: 8350 feet
MAPS: Pike National Forest
    USGS 7.5 Minute Mount Deception, Signal Butte, Westcreek

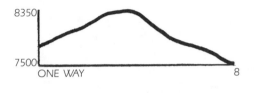

This route begins at the Painted Rocks Campground between Deckers and Woodland Park. It is in an area where there are a lot of other routes to take a shot at. I have written this route description as a one-way ride. You can shuttle a vehicle between Painted Rocks and Westcreek on Hwy. 67. You can also pedal up to Westcreek and return to Painted Rocks the way you came, or you can pedal to Westcreek and pedal back to Painted Rocks on Colorado Hwy. 67. Hwy. 67 is busy. In some places it has little or no shoulder. I would not let kids return this way.

From Woodland Park take Colorado Hwy. 67 north for about 6 miles; turn left at the Painted Rocks Campground entrance—Forest Route 340. You can park along the road or in the campground lot just up the road. The reason for the camp-ground name becomes obvious once you see the rock forma-tions in the area; it's kind of like a mini Garden of the Gods. The nifty top-heavy shapes result from the differential erosion of the different layers of rock. The softer rock erodes faster. Many of these prehistoric monoliths look like they were simply dropped in among the ponderosas.

Begin by pedaling up a slight incline west on Forest Route 340. The road is all-weather gravel. There is some traffic. There are also some private residences along the road. At .5 miles

Forest Route 341, to Quinlan Gulch, intersects 340 from the left. If you want to explore a bit, or add a couple miles to the above trip mileage, you can take 341 until you hit a private area about a mile up the road. Back at the intersection of 340 and 341, follow the sign and 340 toward Westcreek.

Keep climbing past a cattle guard at 1.2 miles and continue past a few private homes. There is a moderate decline at 1.6 miles followed by about a half mile of 10-20 percent climb at 2.2 miles. At 2.6 miles you will come to an intersection with Forest Route 391. Proceed straight ahead; do not turn left. Cruise down a moderate decline through aspen, Douglas fir, and blue spruce. The road conditions are fine. At 3.7 miles the road levels off and continues along West Creek. West Creek contains small brook and rainbow trout.

Pedal past some old deserted log buildings at around 4.4 miles and continue on a series of easy ups and downs. The road narrows after 5 miles as you pedal through the rocks. Pass Douglas County 64 at 6.4 miles and Douglas County 68 at 7 miles; keep going straight ahead toward Westcreek. The road gets wider and more houses pop up as the end gets near.

There is an unmarked intersection at 7.7 miles; turn right. This unmarked road takes you to Colorado Hwy. 67 at about 8 miles.

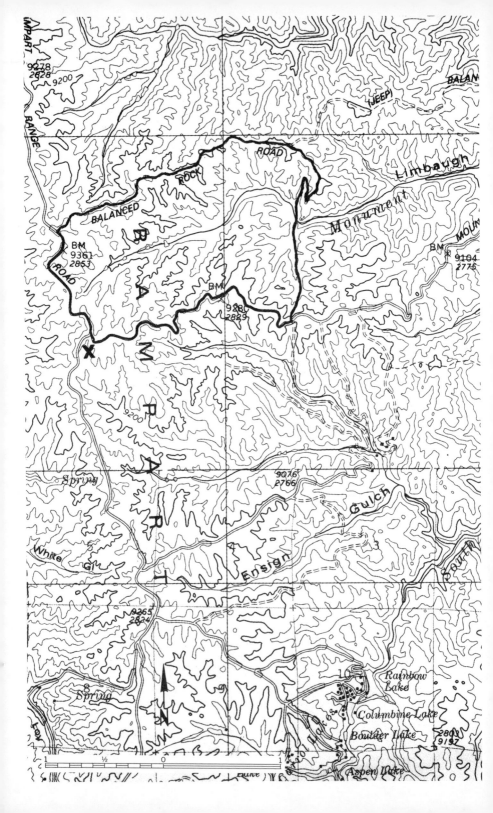

Monument Creek Loop **30**

RIDE RATING: Moderate
SKILL LEVEL: Beginning
ROUND TRIP: 7.5 miles
APPROXIMATE RIDE TIME: 1 hour
STARTING ELEVATION: 9400 feet
HIGHEST POINT: 9400 feet
MAPS: Pike National Forest
    USGS 7.5 Minute Mount Deception, Palmer Lake

9400
9100
ROUND TRIP   7.5

This is a Rampart Range ride. This area, north of Woodland Park, is popular with motorcycle and ATV riders, but this particular tour is on roads that are apparently not as popular with these folks. On an after-supper tour I didn't see a single motorized vehicle.

From Colorado Springs, take U.S. Hwy. 24 to Woodland Park. As you enter Woodland Park, watch for Pikes Peak Road; it's not well marked. In 1986 it was just past a Diamond Shamrock service station on the right side of the road. Turn right on Pikes Peak Road and continue to Baldwin Street. Turn left on Baldwin Street and proceed past the high school. Baldwin becomes Rampart Range Road. About 3 miles from Hwy. 24, there is an intersection where there is a sign that says Rampart Range Road 1 mile; turn to the left and continue past the road to the Rampart Reservoir and follow the signs toward Denver. You are now on the north fork of Rampart Range Road. In another 2 miles or so you will come to the intersection with Mt. Herman Road, the road to Monument. This is the place. Make a right, park along the road, unload, and head toward Monument on Mt. Herman Road, Forest Route 320.

The sign reads "DANGER—NARROW WINDING MOUNTAIN ROAD." It's really not that bad. This is an all-weather gravel road. Start up a moderate grade and after .2 miles begin an easy 1 mile descent. This is one of the few rides that you'll start out going down; it's kind of like opening the bottom of the Crackerjack box first. If you build up a little speed you can

143

stay in high gear and climb up to the lookout at 1.4 miles. At 2.3 miles you will come to the intersection with Forest Route 322.1; turn left onto 322.1 and continue through the trees. The road is narrow and curvy; not bad though. The Air Force Academy is about 5 miles southeast of this point.

You'll need to climb a moderate grade at 3.2 miles that builds up to a 20 percenter at 3.4 miles and then turns into a rollercoaster series of ups and downs. Stay to the left on 322.1 at 3.9 miles. Forest Route 322.1 joins Forest Route 322 at around 4 miles. Route 322 is Balanced Rock Road. Turn left onto 322. You can only go left; to the right is the Palmer Lake Watershed and a closed road.

There is a grand view of Pikes Peak just after you make the turn onto 322. You'll see Pikes Peak for the next couple of miles.

There is some loose gravel on the road, but it is generally in pretty good shape. You'll have easy ups and downs all the way to Rampart Range Road at 6.2 miles. At Rampart Range Road make a left and proceed on a rolling, wide, gravel road back to the start.

Appendix 1

Rank By Ride Rating

ROUTE	RIDE RATING	SKILL LEVEL	PAGE
Wellington Lake Loop	Easy	Beginning	71
Sunlight to Baylor Park	Easy	Beginning	85
Seedhouse Road	Easy	Beginning	41
Grand Mesa Loop	Easy	Begin/Inter	93
St Louis Ck/Fraser Experimental Forest	Easy/Mod	Beginning	33
Vasquez Creek	Easy/Mod	Intermediate	37
Silver Pick Road/ Fall Creek Road	Moderate	Beginning	125
Painted Rocks CG to Westcreek	Moderate	Beginning	139
Monument Creek Loop	Moderate	Beginning	143
Monument Hill	Moderate	Beginning	133
Kebler Pass	Moderate	Beginning	111
Buena Vista to Taylor Pk Reservoir	Moderate	Beginning	119
Buffalo Creek Loop	Moderate	Beginning	75
Como to Breckenridge	Moderate	Begin/Inter	59
Alta	Moderate	Intermediate	129
Rock Creek Ski Road	Moderate	Intermediate	29
Schofield Pass	Moderate	Intermediate	103
Old Fall River Road Loop	Mod/Stren	Beginning	17
Lands End	Mod/Stren	Begin/Inter	89
Slate River/Washington Gulch Loop	Mod/Stren	Intermediate	107
Walton Peak	Mod/Stren	Intermediate	45
Breakneck Pass Loop	Mod/Stren	Intermediate	67
Kite Lake	Mod/Stren	Intermediate	63

Appendix 2

Other Rides By Zone

The following route listing is the result of suggestions and recommendations from various mountain bike shops, guides, and from several of the National Forest district and regional offices. Each route is at least a two-path road. Frequently there are several other good mountain biking roads in the vicinity of each route.

These routes range from Easy and Beginning to Strenuous and Advanced. If you are not familiar with a given route, check with a local mountain bike shop or with the local Forest Service office for the exact route location and an idea of the terrain. It's a good idea to have a good topo map; look for one that covers more than one 7.5-minute quad.

RT. #	ROUTE	COUNTY	NATIONAL FOREST MAP
ZONE 1			
1	Storm Mountain	Larimer	Roosevelt
2	Pole Hill Road/ Panorama Peak	Larimer	Roosevelt
3	Middle St. Vrain	Larimer	Roosevelt
4	Rollins Pass	Boulder/Grand	Roos/Arapaho
5	Rogers Pass	Gilpin/Grand	Roos/Arapaho
6	Apex	Clear Creek	Arapaho
7	Gilpin	Gilpin	Roosevelt
8	Hahns Peak/ Steamboat Lake	Routt	Routt
9	Buffalo Pass	Routt	Routt
10	Dumont Lake Loop	Grand	Routt

RT. #	ROUTE	COUNTY	NATIONAL FOREST MAP
ZONE 2			
11	Red and White Mountain	Eagle	White River
12	No Name Gulch/ Camp Hale Area	Eagle	White River
13	Hagerman Pass	Lake/Pitkin	White Riv/ San Isa
14	Crystal Creek/ Spruce Creek Rd	Summit	Arapaho
15	Mosquito Pass	Park/Lake	San Isabel
16	Browns Pass	Park	Pike
17	Weston Pass	Park/Lake	Pike/San Isa
18	Waldorf	Clear Creek	Arapaho
19	Peru Creek	Summit	Arapaho
20	Saints John	Summit	Arapaho
21	Radical Hill/Deer Creek	Summit	Arapaho
22	Georgia Pass	Summit/Park	Arapaho
23	Mt Falcon	Jefferson	Arapaho
ZONE 3			
24	Windy Point	Garfield	White River
25	Grand Mesa	Mesa/Delta	Grand Mesa
26	Red Table Mountain	Eagle	White River
27	Sopris Creek/Dinkle Lake	Pitkin	White River
28	Capitol Creek/ Montezuma Rd	Pitkin	White River
29	Lenado Rd	Pitkin	White River
30	Mt Yeckel	Pitkin	White River
31	Owl Creek Rd	Pitkin	White River
32	Midnight Mine Rd	Pitkin	White River
33	Smuggler Mtn Rd/ Warren Lakes	Pitkin	White River
34	Little Anne Rd	Pitkin	White River

RT. #	ROUTE	COUNTY	NATIONAL FOREST MAP
ZONE 3 cont'd.			
35	Aspen Mtn to Ashcroft	Pitkin	White River
36	Lincoln Creek Rd	Pitkin	White River
37	Taylor Pass	Pitkin	White River
ZONE 4			
38	Paradise Divide	Gunnison	Gunnison
39	Gunsight Pass	Gunnison	Gunnison
40	Cement Creek	Gunnison	Gunnison
41	Cumberland Pass	Gunnison	Gunnison
42	Tincup Pass	Chaffee/Gunn	Gunn/ San Isabel
43	Saint Elmo	Chaffee	San Isabel
44	Tenderfoot Hill	Chaffee	San Isabel
45	Handcock Pass	Chaffee/Gunn	Gunn/ San Isabel
46	Black Sage Pass	Gunnison	Gunnison
47	Dutchman Creek	Saguache	Gunnison
48	Long Branch	Saguache	Gunnison
49	Marshall Creek	Saguache	Gunnison
50	Marshall Pass	Chaffee/Sagu	Gunn/ San Isabel
51	Los Pinos Pass	Saguache	Gunnison
52	Cochetopa Pass	Saguache	Gunn/Rio Grande
ZONE 5			
53	Sneffels	Ouray	Uncompahgre
54	Imogene Pass	Ouray	Uncompahgre
55	Corkscrew Gulch	Ouray	Uncompahgre
56	Engineer Pass	Ouray/Hinsdale	Uncompahgre
57	Cinnamon Pass	San Juan/Hinsdale	Uncompahgre

RT. #	ROUTE	COUNTY	NATIONAL FOREST MAP

ZONE 5 cont'd.

58	Bear Creek	San Miguel	Uncompahgre
59	Ophir Pass	San Juan/San Mig	San Juan/ Uncom
60	Gladstone	San Juan	Uncompahgre
61	Bolam Pass	Dolores/San Juan	San Juan
62	Mineral Creek	San Juan	San Juan
63	Henderson Lake	La Plata	San Juan
64	Kennebec Pass	La Plata	San Juan
65	Perins Peak	La Plata	San Juan
66	Devil Mountain	Archuleta	San Juan
67	Summitville	Rio Grande	Rio Grande
68	Elwood Pass	Mineral/Rio Grande	Rio Grande
69	Stunner Pass	Rio Grande	Rio Grande
70	Cumbres Pass	Conejos	Rio Grande

ZONE 6

71	Cripple Creek	Teller	Pike
72	Clyde	Teller	Pike
73	Hayden Pass	Fremont/Saguache	Rio Grd/ San Isa
74	Hermit Pass	Custer/Saguache	Rio Grd/ San Isa
75	Querida	Custer	San Isabel
76	Rosita	Custer	San Isabel
77	Music Pass	Custer/Saguache	Rio Grd/ San Isa
78	Mosca Pass	Alamosa/Huerfano	Rio Grd/ San Isa
79	Pass Creek Pass	Huerfano/Costilla	San Isabel
80	Apishapa/Cordova Pass	Las Animas	San Isabel

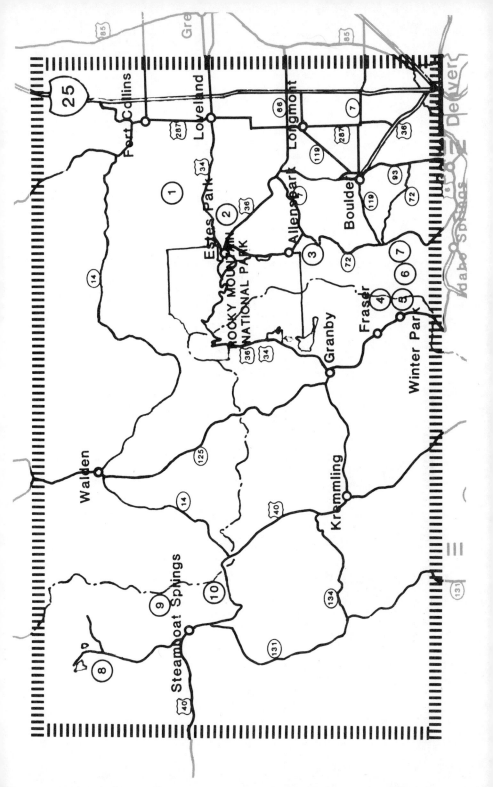

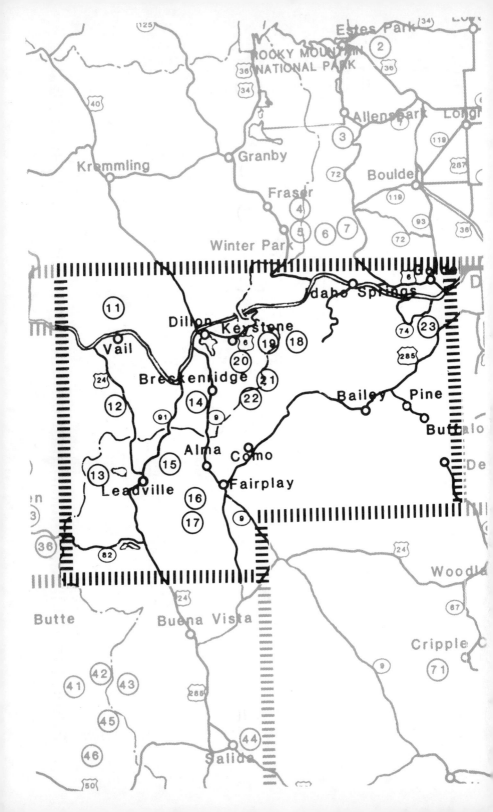

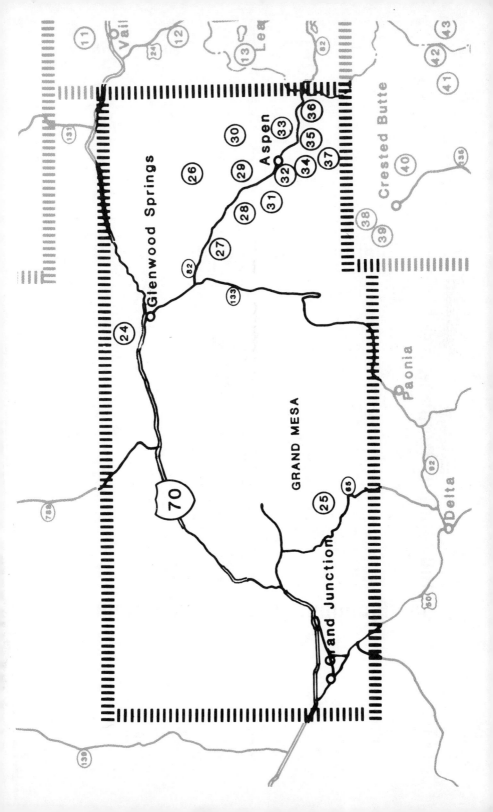

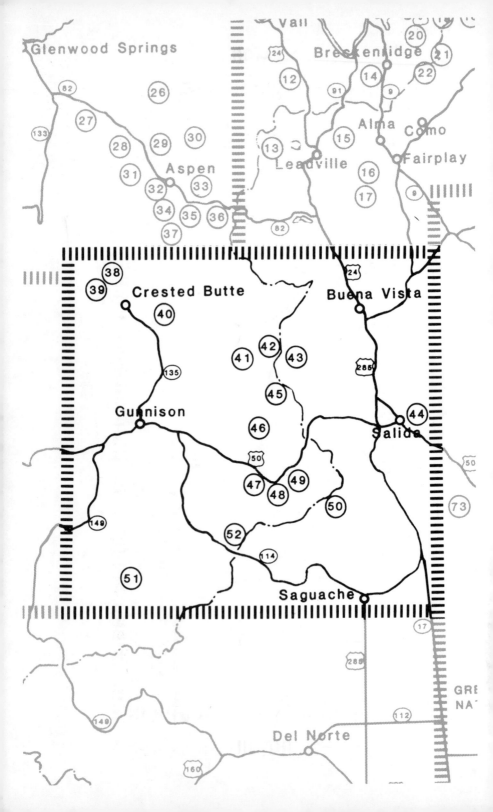

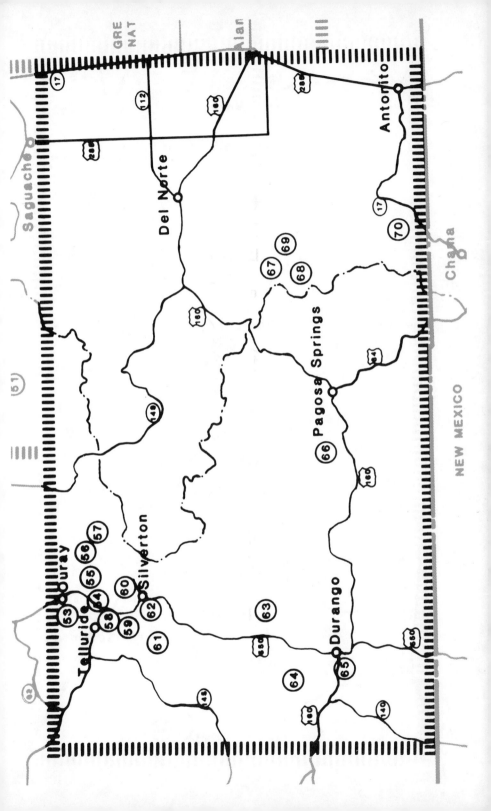

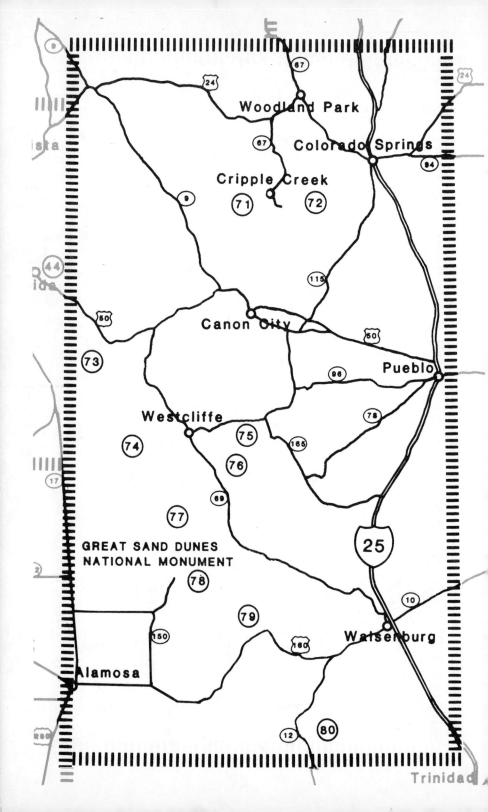